PHOTOGRAPHY BUSINESS

Build a Profitable Photography Business Today

(A Complete Beginner's Guide to Making Money Online With Your Camera)

Brenda Patrick

Published By **Brenda Patrick**

Brenda Patrick

Photography Business: Build a Profitable Photography Business Today (A Complete Beginner's Guide to Making Money Online With Your Camera)

ISBN 978-1-77485-438-9

Legal & Disclaimer

Upon using the information contained in this book, you agree to hold harmless the Author from and against any damages, costs, and expenses, including any legal fees potentially resulting from the application of any of the information provided by this guide. This disclaimer applies to any damages or injury caused by the use and application, whether directly or indirectly, of any advice or information presented, whether for breach of contract, tort, negligence, personal injury, criminal intent, or under any other cause of action.

You agree to accept all risks of using the information presented inside this book. You need to consult a professional medical practitioner in order to ensure you are both able and healthy enough to participate in this program.

TABLE OF CONTENTS

Introduction

Photography is among the most satisfying, artistic, profitable and demanding art forms. Although recording photos for posterity was used since the beginning of time and was only practiced by a select few, the current age and the advancement of technology has made photography to be a hobby that is accessible to everyone. There is no other technology that has created more opportunities for photography than digital cameras.

Although cameras come in a variety of dimensions, shapes, and capacities and capacities, digital cameras are able to make a beginner photographer look like an expert by making just a few adjustments. Anyone who is an experienced photographer will agree that digital cameras are one of the most effective equipment for them as well as those who are not as experienced in their hobby. If you're a novice or a professional photographer, cameras with digital sensors could be among your top and most important options.

Although photography is an art form, there are still rules of science which govern its expression. While the artistic aspects of photography is attainable through the photographer's imagination as well as passion and individual expressiveness, the more technical aspect must be mastered. Only after the fundamentals of a camera have been trained can a photographer use their tools to their maximum potential. When creativity and imagination are combined along with technological advancements, the outcome are bound to be one of the most inspiring, stimulating and, most importantly, lasting art works of our time.

This complete guide will present you with all aspects of photography. It covers various subjects for beginners, as well as specific or advanced topics for those who are experts. From the most basic components of your camera to the often ignored aspects, from a quick introduction to photography, to contemporary trends and tips of photography in the present and from one example after the next to illustrate the practical applications of the most important photography courses This book certainly offers something for anyone who is a photographer.

Chapter 1: Define Your Mission And Set Goals

A social experiment was conducted. In the experiment, participants were put into a large room. In the beginning of the experimentation, participants were instructed to "just begin walking". The researcher put an armchair directly in front of the participants. every time the participants were told to stop walking.

However, during the second phase of the test, they received different instructions. Instead of "just begin strolling" they were instructed to select a specific location and then begin walking toward it. When they saw a chair before them, they didn't stop, or found their way around the chair or removed the chair from their way to get to the place they were headed.

Do you understand what transpired in this instance? Do you realize what changes were created? In the initial round of experiments, they did not have a specific goal in their mind, and so whenever an obstacle came in their path for example, an armchair, it caused them stop moving.

However, even when they set a goal of where they would go and the obstacles didn't hinder them from reaching their goal.

What's the lesson to be learned from this? Focus and gain clarity on your goals.

This will be the initial important aspect in your photography business.

The majority of people don't have an enterprise that will change their lives because they haven't set the goal of having an impactful business. That's fine however, down the line you'll be looking back and regret not having created this opportunity.

It will be apparent the fact that this publication is just as an exercise in self-improvement in business and self-improvement as it does taking photos.

This is one of the greatest lessons I've learned from growing any company, regardless of what it is.

Clarity is essential to any business venture that is successful. You require clarity. You'll need a vision as well as the mission.

Here's the most accurate definition of success I've seen:

"Success is the continuous improvement towards a set objective"

If there's lack of clarity about the desired goal, there will be no actions taken and no results will be achieved.

The first step in achieving what you want from life is... first... to figure out what you desire from your life!

This is among the most profound lessons I've ever learned: how powerful clarity can be.

Clarity will open doors for you.

The more precise you are about your goals, the more likely you are to achieve an amazing result.

There isn't always clarity about the best way to get there but clarity on what you are looking for, and why you'd like it.

When your vision of a goal is sufficiently clear, the road begins to follow itself.

Now, I'll assist you in determining exactly what you'd like from your life. Have you ever tried a car out and thought about buying it? Then you see that vehicle everywhere in town? It wasn't an upswing of people who bought the car, it was just that the awareness of you was increased.

Once you have a clear idea of what you want , you begin looking for people and pathways that can help you achieve the results you desire.

When you're starting something new the first step is to determine your purpose and your motive or reason.

What is the reason you would like to take this step? What is it that this means to you? It's powerful to be able to recall If your motivation is compelling enough, you can discover a way to accomplish it.

One of the top business consultants has written an excellent book called start with the why. In the book Simon Sinek talks about how the most successful companies begin by explaining the reasons behind the things they do. Others start with their mission statement.

For example , company A says"We make great sofas Purchase them!

Then on the other side, the company B states"We believe in being at ease at home, and we believe in keeping the customer in mind. We create great sofas, purchase them!

The best companies and individuals start by asking why. Normal companies and individuals begin by asking what..

In your business, you have to consider the following questions: Why should I start this venture? What are the reasons I'd like to succeed? The more specific and deep the motivation, the more effective! Keep digging until you feel something in you...the more you inquire, the more you'll be able to understand your own.

Perhaps you want to earn $10,000 per monthly.. The reason? Because you want to feel relaxed... Why? Because as you grew as a child, your parents didn't have enough.. You want more for yourself and your children.

When you've gotten deep enough, you'll be able to tell. Do you desire to impress your mother? Are you looking to prove the world that is worth something? Do you wish to look after your children better than parents cared for you? Always ask yourself why.

My first mentor said to me that when your motivation doesn't make you cry, then it's not strong enough.

My mentor at first, Chad, was raised by a single mother who had to go away to work in order to be able to take care of all five boys on her own. His childhood was okay however he observed youngsters from his neighborhood doing things that they weren't capable of doing. Mom was absent often and he never had the chance to go on take a vacation.

The brother who was Chad's was injured and broke the leg of one brother.. The next night, Chad was walking down the hallway when he was convinced that his mother was crying. He went into her room. He saw his mother kneeling on her knees and crying in her arms.. She was unable to take on the world as it was, and her broken leg was pushing her to the edge. That was Chad's motivation for why his goal was to be successful. The next night, he had an open fire that was lit beneath his feet.

He wanted to care for his mother. He wanted to be proud of her. If he was a father and a home, he didn't want to put his children in this circumstance. When I hear him tell me about this experience, tears well up in his eyes.

The speed was up by 20 years, Chad was able to purchase his mother a modest house, one in which the pipes that were in place before wouldn't be breaking. Chad had a compelling reason and that helped him through the ups and downs of life.

If you're really serious about it then sit down and be real to yourself over a short period of time. Discover the reasons you desire to see this happen. Go as deep as you can. Even if it's just a superficial motive, at least you've got a reason. However, we all have some reason.

If you've identified your reason now is the time to get crystal-clear on what you want to accomplish.

What are you looking for? What are your objectives to help you realize your purpose come true.

You may need more time, money and freedom, or whatever is important to you.

Imagine that you're sitting on this spot twelve months from today. What are you hoping to be? What are you proud of? What are you doing that you do not currently have? Perhaps you'd like to be healthier, or maybe you'd like more money, or perhaps you're looking to start a family or perhaps you'd like to establish a profitable photography business. Draw a vivid picture of your personality and the things you've achieved. Who are you working with? What number is on your account in the bank? What are you hoping to influence your client's life? What does your social media appearance like? What is your location?

List what you'd like to get completed in the next twelve months. Make sure you don't miss a single details! If you are excited by something take note of it! The higher your ambitions, the greater impact you'll have within your own life as well as your friends and family! If you're like the majority of people, you'd like to 1. To feel healthier and more satisfied 2. To build stronger relationships 3. To have more impact 4. To earn more. The best part is that the blueprint I'm going to share with you will assist you by completing at least 3 of those four aspects. The time is short, so make time to complete this task of deciding on where you'd like to be and it will assist you in achieving what you want from your life. Decide now to answer this question and note it down in a way that you can look at it daily "what do I want to be able to achieve within the next 12 months?"

Once you've identified what you're looking for It's time to take a step back and look at where you're at currently. If you're looking to earn $10,000 per month, what's the amount you're earning right now? If you're planning to work just 15 hours per week, what are you doing now? If you plan to travel once every two months What is the frequency you currently travel?

It's time to determine the roadblocks that are currently in place. The most common roadblocks that I observe people having are: 1. They lack clarity about what they want to do (if you've completed the exercise mentioned above, you've got more certainty in your life than the vast majority of people) 2. The third most frequent issue is that people don't have a proper blueprint to follow and third. They don't have the appropriate people in their lives. The rest of this book will provide you with the guidelines to success and bring the right people into your life. Your job is to follow the steps you learn from this book!

Here are some essential guidelines to keep in mind to help you with your work as you move forward.

1. You will always be able to make more money, but you'll never have more time. Time is among many secrets that make the successful. They invest money to make more time, and to increase their productivity. The more you consider your time more important than your money ,

the more content you'll beand the more freedom you'll enjoy and the more money you'll be earning.

This was apparent when my wife edited pictures on her laptop. She was editing her photos using this laptop and it was incredibly slow! I'm talking about it was incredibly slow! It was almost painful to see her edit and lose the time. It took a few days to finish with editing one photoshoot.

When I asked her about it, she said that ever she's thought about getting an upgrade to her laptop.. It should be faster that allows her to edit images quickly. This means she's able to use her most valuable resource and time on other things. She replied that "it's acceptable, it'd be too expensive to purchase an entirely new laptop. It's not worth it". A few months later, I purchased her a new laptop for Christmas. (cant resist this!)

She was elated but unsure whether this was a smart purchase. After she booked and completed her subsequent shoots the difference was evident. She was able finish editing in just one-fourth of what it could take.

The editing time she was able to cut from 12 hours for each shoot to about two or three hours. She invested that time in increasing her client base, which resulted in her being paid more often and gave her better practice. This made her better. This resulted in her charging higher per customer, which resulted in better results. Also, getting more clients also brought in new clients.

The reason is that it occurred when we took out the bottleneck in her work that was a time squanderer due to the computer's slow speed. While it may not be my wife's initial choice, the investment in the speedier computer cost it 100 times over.

Speedmeans lesser work= less practicewhich means less results and a lesser impact on the world as well as your personal life. If you value money over your time Your time will always be less valuable than your money. However, once you change your mindset and consider your time to be more valuable than your money Your value of time can be more than your money and as a result, you'll make more money and will have more time.

Remember that your time is the most important asset. It is possible to always earn more money, but not more time, therefore, be willing to pay for more time. This will return 100 times your investment. 2. Always keep learning This book is just a small portion the journey. You'll want to master an idea. Learn it, practice and repeat. Your abilities will be sharper and more sharp when you practice by practicing and repeating.

Another method to accelerate your progress is to be around people who run the kind of business you want to run. Check out how they run it. What they do with their amazing images that attract customers and how they price what they charge, from where they're from, and where they intend on taking their business. After that, you try the things you've learned, and when you've reached your level take a look at more. It's true that you only gain so much from one source, so you must always be studying.

3. If you're looking to become extremely successful, you must concentrate on marketing. Is it true that McDonalds serve the most delicious hamburgers in town? Nearly all the time it is not. However, even if McDonalds isn't the best hamburgers in town What makes them succeeding?

Here's the solution. They're not in business of producing hamburgers, they're involved in making and selling hamburgers!

If you're not involved in making pictures, but rather engaged in market and selling products. To be a professional photographer, you must take great photos. is a significant part of the puzzle however it's not the only piece of the picture.

It is essential to know how to share and market your work to have a massive impact. To this end, this book will not only assist you take amazing photos however, it will also assist you in marketing your amazing photos to gain more customers.

4. This is the final principle to look at your business from. To boost your business's value, you must improve the value of your business. It is impossible to pretend to be great. The world won't give you anything greater than you are, so you must do something everyday to boost your worth, improve your capabilities and help you become a better person.

More important than anything your actions are is what you.

The most valuable people are special and incomparable. In the final analysis, people will pay the price for you as a person and not just for the things you do.

Be someone of high value, one who gives before receiving and you'll be content, happy and get great things in your work and in life. Your worth is enhanced by practicing, and becoming an irreplaceable human being.

After we've gotten some of the mental shifts that you must make to get your photography business going we can get into some of the real techniques and steps you can begin taking today to make your photography business to work to your advantage!..

Chapter 2: What The Dslr Operates

Your image is viewed through the viewfinder. This is a small hole on the back of the camera that lets you can see the image you wish to take. Light is reflected off the mirror by the lens. The pentaprism then transforms vertical light into horizontal light, and directs it towards the viewfinder. The pentaprism is situated within your camera, right behind the lens and shutter.

After you have taken your photo when you press on the shutter button mirror is moved up to allow light to pass through. This also stops the channel in the vertical direction,, and then the shutter is opened and light hits the sensor. The shutter is closed and causes the mirror reflex to rotate forward.

If you've got some basic knowledge of how DSLRs function You'll probably be interested in knowing how to take beautiful photos using the triangle of exposure to the maximum.

How to compose great photos

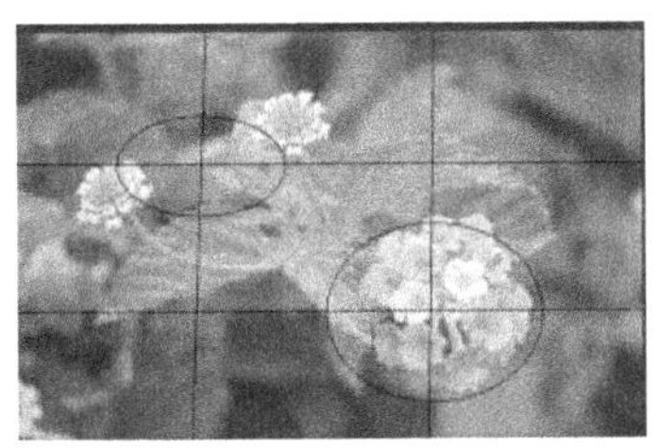

Top Composition Rules

A Rule of Thirds

Following the rule of thirds makes sure that your photo is interesting for the viewers. Imagine that the image you want to show is divided into 9 equal pieces, with two horizontal and two vertical lines. It is known that placing your photo in the middle of these lines can create more attraction, rather than centered. It helps create balanced image. Actually, the rule is so popular in photography today that certain camera makers have added features to allow users to take pictures in this way, without having to apply it on your head. The cameras have an option to superimpose grid lines on your image prior to taking the photo. If you're using a camera with this feature make sure to position the image in the intersection of these horizontal and vertical lines, and then compare it with other images that you do not.

Beware of the Centre

The tendency among photographers who are new to photography to position all their photos in the middle of their frame. If you were to look over some of the more captivating images in magazines, newspapers and even on the internet you'll find that professional photographers attempt to stay clear of the center in every way they can. A photo that is placed in the center might seem like it's your primary goal, however it's a dull method of doing it. While straying away from the center of the image, like using rules of thirds appears to create a gap in the center however, you can fill in this empty space by adding something of lesser importance within the photograph. This method is efficient in using rules of thirds, and solving the central emptyness issue.

Get Closer to your Image

The closer you get to your object of your interest can help to take clear images. It also makes it easier to remove what you don't require from the photograph.

Reduce the Scene

The main reason behind every shot is the subject matter. It is therefore crucial to choose your subject in order you can only use images that tell the main story about the topic. Make sure you select settings that are focused on the subject, and are able to distinguish different objects. After you've selected your object of interest, and then picked a zoom that is suitable (depending on the lens) Try to put the other objects to the background of the image, or to push them out of the frame. If you are not keen to include other objects in the background or eliminate them altogether, make them a part of the story that you are telling through your subject.

It is crucial to know that simplifying your photo's scene can help your photographs have a distinct subject. It's a great method to reduce clutter in photography. It is not a good idea to capture photos that leave viewers wondering what exactly they're supposed to be seeing. Your image should be able to speak by it's own. In any event it is unlikely that you'll have to clarify what you were trying to achieve. It is essential to be able to live up to the fame of your photo. There is a saying that says a photograph speaks a thousand words, so keep the space in your print with beautifully taken photos that have distinct concepts.

Fill in the Frame

Frames are what surround your focal point in a photograph. By filling in the frame of your photo creates the right balance between utility and. By filling the frame you can make the subject of your photograph appear bigger while ensuring there is less clutter and distractions within the photograph. Voids act as detractors in photography. The issue of having empty space within a frame is a major challenge should you try to tackle it by yourself. A very frequent aspects of empty space is skyless skies. Naturally, the absence of clouds reduces the size of the object; thus making it less attractive to the observer. This is a challenging scenario to manage since you might not have the the option of dealing with it when making the photo. Even though you have the option of using post-processing software to alter and improve your photographs You can minimize this nuisance or eliminate it altogether by moving closer or zooming in to the object you want to photograph. Zooming in can give you a better perspective of the photo in front of you. Zooming in closer exposes more details and makes your photo more appealing to look at. This option is only available when you have the chance and freedom to freely move within your subject. If not, the post-processing option will be the image salvager.

Use Leading Lines

The concept of lines may be a bit confusing for beginners, but it's simple enough to grasp in the course of a few attempts. The lines used in photography aren't actually lines like we would recognize them in everyday language, but photographs, the objects with forms that are linear within the backgrounds are described as lines. There are a variety of lines that we can use in photography. Examples include electricity lines, buildings lines roads, walls, fences, etc. The geometric shapes can be varied and of course, deliver various results. They could be wavy straight lines or curving. It is also contingent on your intent to capture the image. For example vertical lines usually convey the feeling of performance peace, power and strength. They also convey height as well as dominance, strength, integrity, substance, and so on. while horizontal lines communicate an impression of calm as well as calm, width stability and security. They also convey a sense of constancy, stability, and security. It has been proven that lines aid in guiding viewers in a specific direction. While you are viewing the image through the viewfinder on your camera, make sure to align the image with these lines to ensure that your pictures do not seem out of alignment to their surroundings.

The main purpose of the lines is to focus the eye of the eye. You can also make an imaginary line which successfully helps to focus. For instance, using an image that is off center and is facing in a specific direction could lead the user to the goal.

If you are planning to use leading lines, make sure that you utilize a small apertures to make a deep depth of field that everything that must be visible in the photo into focus. When using leading lines, you're most likely to shift the eye towards the background objects in the picture. Therefore, you need to ensure that the objects on the background are in focus. By using leading lines, you are able to:

*Lead a person to move from one object in the image to the next

Make sure to keep the eye of the viewer's attention on a specific area of the photograph.

Use Diagonals

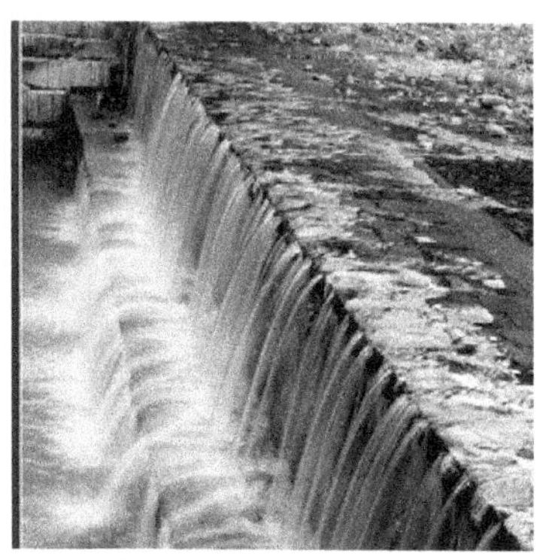

In addition, lines serve more than leading the viewer to an object that is interesting in a photo. Lines can also create effects. You can make use of them to convey your story. Horizontal lines give a tranquil and static look. These lines can be used to create an extremely powerful sense of motion or depth. Vertical lines convey a sense of stability and permanence while diagonals are the best choice for creating an impression of action and drama. They create a sense movement and the feeling of uncertainty. These effects add tremendous value to your photos. Although you aren't required to have these effects in one photograph You have the option to pick one that can effectively convey your message, and then transmit the message to the viewer with no stress. You can achieve diagonal lines using tilting your camera a bit to switch vertical and horizontal lines into horizontal ones so that you can get the desired effect. You could also apply the zig-zag effect when you're using diagonals when creating patterns. If repeated the patterns you aid in bringing your eyes to the image across a wider space within the frame.

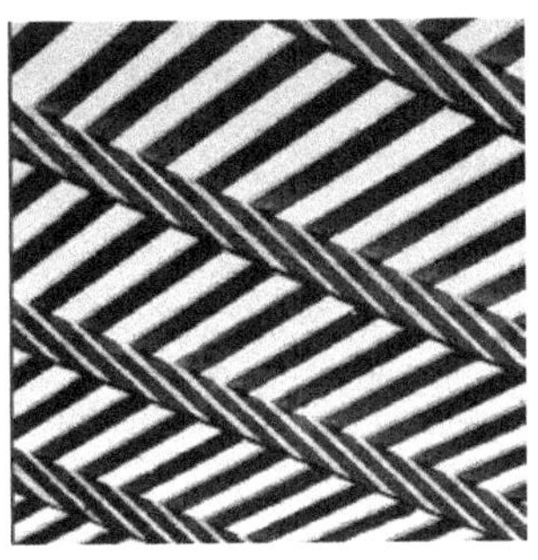

You can enjoy wider angles of view using broad angle lens. Through these lens, you will have the option of tilting and move to get a better view than the scene you want to see.

Dutch Tilt Technique Dutch Tilt Technique

This technique lets you can create unique angles by tilting slowly the camera as you snap the photograph. The photos that result are typically distinctive and convey special emotions.

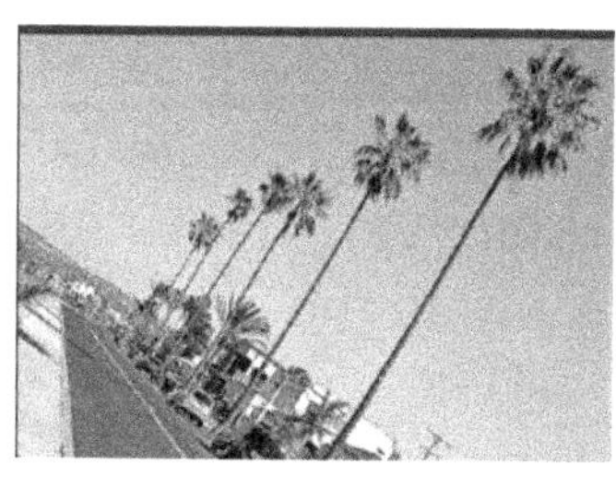

Create Space to Move

A well-crafted photo conveys an impression of motion. You can create a sense in your photographs by making sure the subject is given enough space to move around, typically in front of them. This can be achieved by first making sure that your subject isn't in close proximity to the frame.

If you are able to look at the photos that we see on a daily basis, like those that are on billboards, the clever creating of space for subjects allows us to follow the motion or gaze of their subject. The subject must have the space to look around or move around, since it adds life to the picture and reduces the impression of a static scene. It is recommended to make more space before the photograph than behind.

Backgrounds

Backgrounds can ruin or enhance your photograph. Therefore, you must be aware and aware of what will allow as background for your photo. Unorganized backgrounds ruin your photo. It is possible to discern what is visible in the background by adjusting the angle of view and changing the location. A wide aperture lens can be a useful aid in deciding what objects that should be included within the background.

You can also use using the zoom function to move the unwanted objects out of the frame. Also, the choice of a background must be determined by the story you intend to tell. Determine if a background is needed to be a part of the tale or not.

Colors

While primary colors work in getting attention, they've been utilized for a long time across a wide range of topics. It is possible to take a different method by splashing color onto the monochromatic background. The key to successful color manipulation is in your ability to distinguish and frame subjects in a distinctive way.

Do not be afraid to break the rules

If you're aware of that you must follow the guidelines, then could be forced to break them in a moment. However, it's essential to know the rules you must break in a particular scene. While rules have shaped photography throughout the years and provided a foundation to establish photography as a distinct discipline that is based on a corpus of information The beauty of photography is also in breaking away from the conventional and accepting spontaneity.

It's not unusual to come across stunning photographs which haven't abided by all the rules. However, it is crucial to learn the rules to be able to violate them to achieve a goal. Most often, the images that attract attention are designed to communicate a specific message. So, rather than embarking on a wild-card excursion with your camera be sure to learn the rules first. You can then violate them in order to communicate an idea.

Photography is an artistic process. Similar to other forms of art, spontaneity and creativity are not far from the process. To limit photography using rigid rules is unsustainable. There are plenty of instances where photographers blatantly break the rules, yet still create amazing photos in the end.

Now that you know the important picture composition rules that you need to follow, or break if you feel the need to, let's dive into more details about how to take advantage of the power of framing in order to create the most effective photos that convey precisely what you want to say.

Learn how to make use of the broad appeal

If you're taking portrait photography, it is best to be focusing more on your subject's eyes. By placing them in the center of your image it is likely that you'll find yourself with lots of space in front of the face of the subject. This is why you should try to keep the eye in the upper horizontal direction. In the event that your model is placed on one sideof the frame, ensure that they do not look straight at the edge of the image. Therefore, if they're facing the right-hand part of the image make sure that they're standing on the vertical line so that you can ensure that they look at the space to the right part of the picture.

Don't be shy about using this same method to capture action shots.

Chapter 3: How To Market Your Photographs Online

Selling your photos online can be a challenge however, with the right assistance, you'll be able to ensure that the people you want to attract will be able to view what you are selling as "products" and buy they do not have to travel into your office. Naturally every photographer is able to sign up for a the stock photo membership or set up a website and begin selling their images on the internet, but many of them will not be able to take their businesses to an unimaginable lucrative heights due to the fact that they do not have the necessary knowledge to be sure that they're successful in launching their online business.

Online Photography FAQs

As you are entering this new venture in business there are certain questions you must be able to answer before moving into selling your photos or even your photography service online. These are the questions that newbies in this kind of business often have to ask:

1. How can I make money online using my images?

There are a variety of ways to earn money from the services and photos that you provide online:

A privately owned website or selling platform for photographers create an impressive and appealing portfolio to draw in buyers, but advertisers as well who would like to purchase space on the website.

* Galleries available for direct customers If you'd wish to provide your photography services such as photography classes or photoshoots apart from selling the pictures you've taken, you can create an online gallery with your products and services your prospective customers or patrons directly are likely to see.

* Stock photography is most likely the most popular method of selling your pictures online, particularly for those who don't have enough expertise and are just beginning out, or need to find a faster way to market their pictures. Registration is easy and uploading photos is simpler.

2. How much should I market my images for?

It all depends on the platform you choose. For instance, if you are planning to sell your photographs on your own site You will be able to charge according to the actual cost of taking the pictures in uploading, maintaining and maintaining the website.

However, for those who are looking to sell your photos on marketplaces for stock photos, they may charge less than selling through the gallery you own or on a selling through a selling platform. However, you must be aware that photos that are posted and sold on "stocks" may rise in value based on the amount of downloads. You could make more money if you decide to upload a large quantity of high-quality photos. If, for instance, you're selling your picture at around 25 cents per download you might think it's not much but a number of sales can add up to hundreds of dollars, particularly in the case of photos that are excellent and captivating.

3. What is the best way to get the money for downloads?

Of of course, if you'll sell your photo service and actual images on your own website or platform Your payments can be directed to the preferred online payment service, for example via PayPal and Payoneer or directly through your banking services on the web. However, for stock photo websites there are different rules for payment. Certain sites permit members to make money after they have earned 100 or more. It is possible to be paid by PayPal or by check.

4. What kind of images sell well on the internet?

With time and consistency in the submission of images, you can be able to determine what photos sell and which do not. However, since you're just beginning to develop your photography career online it is important to be aware that, unless you have your own website, the submission or uploading images to stock sites does not guarantee that every single one of them are approved to sell. That means you'll likely be faced with many rejections before you can finally grasp what exactly the process is. It shouldn't be a cause for concern though, since all those who is selling their pictures online will go through this.

For a better understanding Most people look for images that are adaptable, simple to edit and easy to upload to any place. People also like photos that have brighter or whiter backgrounds because they tend to be more traditional and common at times. Images of animals or humans with white backgrounds are sought-after because they are easy to alter and edited "Photoshopped" and superimposed on photos or backgrounds. In addition they can be used with virtually every theme.

Strategies to Market Your Pictures Online Concentrating on a couple of platforms can assist you in selling your images effortlessly. There are many methods you could use to sell your photography services or photographs on the internet, and by researching each one you'll be able to decide which selling platforms or platforms you'd prefer to use.

Selling Images or Photography on your own site

A site and selling platforms will make sure that you make more money as you won't need to give away a part of your sales on photography to stock photo websites. How do you approach this? Here are some tips to keep in mind when selling photos on your own website:

Check if your website is built on the WordPress platform. Once you have this setup, it allows you to access many plug-ins, themes , and designs that enable you to market your photos on your website. The themes and plug-ins you choose to use are very easy to install and put on your site This means you don't have to worry about not being knowledgeable about the technical aspects in web-based development.

Make sure you price your photos according to your needs. Keep your expenses at heart, set your prices for your images in a way that is competitive without losing money. This allows you to go head-to- with those selling their photos at extremely affordable prices. This is especially true in the case of trying to sell stock images on your website.

* Give free downloads This might be a bit odd since you're trying to make some money here. Giving something away for free is an effective marketing tactic since customers are always searching for websites with the most attractive bargains.

* Offer package deals Bundling your stock images together can certainly increase the value of your business. All you have to do is bundle the photos in a certain amount within the same theme. This will make it easier for customers to download your images.

Selling Your Photos via Stock Photo Sites
It is among the most straightforward ways to sell and earn money from photographs you love making. With the increase in writers, bloggers and website owners searching for top images to upload, along

with other content has opened up new opportunities for beginners as well as professionals to market their photos and earn more. So , how do you sell your images on photography websites that sell stock photos?

Join and become an active member. You will not be in a position to sell your photographs via stock websites if aren't a member. It's really simple to sign up as you'll have to provide all the details the site requires. A majority of stock sites are completely free, so paying isn't an issue.

Apply to be an contributor. This will ensure that you be able to submit your images to be approved and sold. It is then your responsibility to study about the best way to submit the photos or upload them to avoid rejection.

Create a photo collection It's not recommended to upload one image per week or day since you will need to submit your images for approval before they can be sold. It is important to create an impressive collection of a large quantity of quality photos to be able to handle potential rejections and increase the chances of sales and uploads. Stock photo websites will are also worth a look the quality as well as quantity to ensure consistency.

* Choose more common and relatable images Keep your more emotionally charged and thought-provoking images for direct or specific customers since you'll be selling stock photos. Use the standard ones but ensure that they're relatable and of the finest quality. Be aware that photos that are simple regardless of what the subject matter is when they are captured and edited beautifully, they can trigger the appropriate reactions and emotions from the intended audience.

Select a reputable micro-stock or third-party stock photo retailer that can easily and swiftly make your pictures available to download and purchase. It also gives your images the right of exposure, especially since you're just beginning to get into your business.

Be prepared to pay commissions. Of course, commissions will be automatically paid every when the photos are sold. photos as you're utilizing an expert service from a third-party seller. Some charge anywhere from 20% to up to 60% commission or royalty from sales of images you've bought through the site.

This won't aid in growing your business, but it will allow you to earn more money beginner photographers looking to make money should consider selling stock images. If you are contemplating the possibility of creating a brand that is well-known, this shouldn't be the only reason they ought to consider selling images online, as you're also competing with other photographers who sell their work. You can create your own website while selling stock photos while also using it to advertise their business.

Selling Your Photos on Your Blog

With the plethora of photographers striving to make their work known it's a challenge to establish your brand quickly. Promoting your company can be difficult because there are just too numerous fish to be found in the water. In reality shining a the spotlight on your business or products and services is similar to trying to find the dark stone within a space saturated with charcoal. Like any other road bump there's a great method to market and promote your brand and photos and we're not only talking of social media advertising. We're also talking about search engine Optimization.

We're talking about blogging!

Blogs are a safer and exciting way for companies to communicate their message. With tons of relevant keywords to the services you offer it will be quite surprising that your website and images are not noticed in any way. To drive people to your site and encourage people to buy your images, you must ensure that you

• Publish regularly content on your blog. People love sharing their life experiences This is the reason blogs are so popular. Let people know how much you enjoy your work, and then share some of your pictures on your blog's page. This will keep your readers engaged and keep your readers coming back to read more.

Link your website blogs are considered as extensions of real websites, meaning that you can connect your blog however you'd like. Be sure to provide a subtle reference to the services you provide to make clients feel like you're not trying to force them to buy your images or purchase your services.

Chapter 4: Winging It: Setting Your Online Portfolio

In contrast to joining and sharing profits on the stock photography sites There are some who wish to create their own website and sell their photographs independently.

It's not a bad idea to begin. It has several advantages over stock websites:

You're in charge. You don't need to get your pictures examined by an editor to determine whether they're worth selling or not. Also, you'll have control of the layout of your site and its overall appearance are the result of your own design.

You get to keep all earnings. Because you don't pay for the image-hosting and marketing, each download you sell goes directly into your account.

You decide the price. If you feel your photograph is worth an amount there is nothing to hinder you from putting it up with the price you want.

You are the one who gets credit as well as the customers. If you encounter clients of your work on the website you're certain to keep them from your site because you won't have to share hosting space with other photographers.

However, just like every other option there are disadvantages also:

You must do the marketing on your own. Like any other business owner it is essential to create the posts yourself, emails blasts, invitations, promotions and even research on competitors.

There is no mentor. You don't have one unless you can find someone within your circle of friends. The stock photography website provides you with an entire community of photographers who can receive assistance. Starting your own website won't open these types of doors for you.

You'll be responsible for your own maintenance of your site. If something breaks it will be your responsibility to take on the task of fixing all the issues unless you have an army of web developers who can make sure that everything is working again.

If you've already made your mind to attempt setting your own site then you could try PhotoShelter like we mentioned previously or use other methods for setting up your website.

Before you start you'll have to learn some basics about the process of setting up an online store for your photos.

What are you looking for?

Alongside a hosting service, you'll have to come up with a payment method that allows your customers to benefit from your efforts.

There's also a way that allows you to place watermarks on your photos. Watermarks are essentially silhouettes of logos, or other images that identify your photos as yours. Keep in mind that unless you plan to distribute your photos to the public for free, you'd better put a watermark on your website. This will keep unscrupulous users from copying the hyperlinks to your website's images and then using your images for free.

Another tool you'll need is a tool to resize your images. This will allow you to view your images in greater resolutions. This is essential since you'll need to make different sizes of your images available to your clients. The greater the resolution, the more the price you will be able to cost. Imagine it as different sizes of sodas in the local fast food restaurant. There are web-based tools to help you reduce the size of your photos or download software for photo editing to do it.

When you have all of these items available, you are able to begin looking for a good host to host your site.

WordPress

You may have heard this phrase when it comes to content creation and blogging on the internet. Most people do not know that the web hosting service of WordPress also provides support to photographers who want to create their own content.

What is it that makes WordPress an excellent host is the accessibility of plug-ins to enhance your site's functionality. Based on the requirements of your site, WordPress has over 25,000 plug-ins to enhance the functionality of your site.

The feature you're searching to find include one of them is the Sell Media plug-in. The installation of this plug-in will enable you to accept payments on your website without the need to build external links that lead users away from the website. It's specially designed to sell images, making it easy to use. It's everything you'd want to have in an extension.

SmugMug

Like PhotoShelter, SmugMug allows you to build a website on your own with some of their template. Additionally, you can integrate e-commerce tools into your website, in order to get money for the use of your images.

One of the things that makes this website stand out from other sites is the marketing tools. Since you'll manage your marketing according to your own preferences they will prove beneficial for you.

With the help of various tools included in your membership, you'll be able to effortlessly share your content on social media platforms to connect with your intended audience. Visitors can make comments about your work, and serve as a useful instrument to evaluate your strengths and weaknesses.

With a professional account you'll have access to additional tools, like visitor analytics and SEO-optimized widgets. Additionally, you'll be able to develop promotions and deals to encourage users to visit your site ahead of your competitors. Additionally, it will allow you to design an image that appears across everything from your website. It will appear on your shopping carts, business cards, and even on your orders. This logo will appear every single item that you show, regardless of what size.

LightRocket

Many photographers who haven't had success on stock photography sites have turned to LightRocket to develop their photography professions. It's one of the few that offer free memberships, which allow users to build their own website and also sell your photos.

The benefits of their free membership aren't too bad, either. The initial 5GB is storage and can link your content to social media websites. There's also a contact list that lets you arrange your clients.

It's the customers that attracted photographers to this site. Many big companies have sought photographers because of their activities on LightRocket. Companies like National Geographic, The New York Times, Forbes, Marie Claire and even Scholastic have reached out to LightRocket to gain access with a photographer due to their content. If you're looking to gain traction here's the place to be.

Both stock photography sites as well as self-published websites have each their own pros and cons, but the choice is entirely yours as the photographer. Some have tried a mix of both approaches to determine which is more profitable, however this takes an enormous amount of work. Many have started out with stock photos and came up with their own websites. It's sometimes the reverse approach.

However, once you've reached your choice, you'll have to learn a few additional suggestions to ensure that you're successful in both.

Chapter 5: Searching For An Agency

It is not necessary to travel to far away and visit actual companies who will accept the contents on your card. Fortunately, Microstock photography can be generally done online. Applications are quick and easy, and the money is deposited automatically.

The first question you'll want to ask is where you should begin your search. This can be answered by taking the time to look through some websites and seeing how they represent their photographers, and understanding their programs. There are many agencies in search of photographers of all levels, whether they are novice or experienced. Here are some great locations to begin with, as well as some details about them.

Shutterstock

It's surprising that it's among the biggest, if not the biggest agencies in the market of online advertising in the present. Their massive database expands by one million images each month. With such a vast collection it's hard to think about how they'll remain on top.

They're also among the few firms that were at the time when the trend began to gain momentum in the early 2000's. To date they're part of the biggest collection of micro stock companies on the market.

The good news is that making a contribution is easy. Their main site is linked to the bottom of their page that lets users to view their contribution programs.

After signing in, you are now able to begin to submit your images and then have them sell your images for the price that you set.

Incredibly, Shutterstock operates on an annual subscription basis. It is an annual fee for a specific time period to join the community. For that period they can download be able to download a specific amount of files each day. This information can be used to establish the appropriate cost. This isn't a "per-download" scheme that lets you and the website receive a specific percentage of the revenue each time a visitor clicks one of your pictures.

Canstockphoto

Canstockphoto also offers subscription programs which charge a set amount for a predetermined amount of time. They also offer per-download options for users with a less budget.

Participating as a contributor is the same procedure similar to Shutterstock. There's a way to become one on their homepage. The site has a useful guide to help you understand what you can expect when you begin your journey. According to the website it is expected that everything will be completed in the course of a day. It is possible to upload images immediately when you've been granted access to the site as contributor.

What's unique about Canstockphoto's referral program is that it rewards contributors. Contributors don't only get paid for their contributions. If you're capable of recommending photographers to them, you'll also be able to earn an additional $5 every time that the photographer is able to sell 50 copies!

iStockphoto

One of the most intriguing aspects of this website is that it is able to sell every resolution available for an image for a fixed price. This can be helpful when making a decision on the price of your inventory.

In addition, iStock is now quite well-known within the realm of Microstock photography since it's an integral part of Getty Images group. If you're new to the business, Getty Images is the largest license company on the market today. The company purchases or works together with Microstock agencies to assist license their assets.

To sign up you must click"Contribute" on the "sell stocks" link that is located at the top of the page. Then it will guide you through the steps to become an contributor. What's unique is that you'll be asked to send a few samples of your work prior to them being able to decide to accept you as an contributor. This way, they will be able to determine if they are interested in the work you've submitted as photographer.

Fotolia

One thing you should be aware of about this website is that your prices rise as your library grows and the popularity of your site. This means that the more people download your images, the higher the rates you will earn!

It involves a lot of sales, and sometimes making it exclusive. This is when you offer the photo exclusively to the agency. Save your top images for them if you believe they'll be a big hit.

They also offer subscription plans for the long-term client who is satisfied with the services they provide.

In addition to these four major names In addition, there are tons of other great places to go to. A quick Google search for stock photography agencies will produce a great list. Each agency has its own policies as compared to the other. This is why it's essential to research a website prior to signing up. There are policies that aren't compatible with your schedule for photography or payment plans that do not work for you.

A decent agency will offer a photographer somewhere between 20cents and 40 cents per download, assuming that it follows the basis of a per-download system. Consider this as a guideline when you're considering signing up with an agency.

It might seem like a tiny starting point but once you've many photos earning significant amounts of money for yourself, it will be well worth it.

What can be Too Much?

As a novice perhaps you are wondering whether joining any agency is the right option. While you can get plenty of exposure through various websites but getting in every crevice and crevice on the internet might not be the most effective option.

It is possible that your stock photos will be more popular when you are a part of multiple agencies, but this could reduce your earnings potential also. If your photos are listed distributed across multiple websites with different payment options There is a high chance that the downloads originate from less-paying companies instead of higher-paying ones.

It's also time-consuming. Each image you submit has to be classified and labeled with keywords prior to being licensed and distributed to the general public. Imagine being in 10 different agencies. It would be necessary upload, search and tag a group of images ten times before you could call it the day.

In addition it is possible to be rejected by your agency and you will have to cover the shortfall by the process of cleaning up your image. This will cost you a lot of time you could have been able to spend on taking more stock photos on the job.

This is the reason the amount of agencies that you are a part of is an individual preference. Are you prepared to handle the variety of duties which comes with being member of a variety of agencies? Are you able to manage that along with your day-to-day job?

In this situation it is essential to find the ideal balance between comfort and efficiency. Excessive effort at the beginning can cause you to be exhausted early in the game, particularly when the income is low.

It is best to begin with two or three agencies. It's a small number which still provides enough exposure to the biggest stock photography markets worldwide.

Some Important Reminders
In addition to finding a great site to sell your inventory It is also essential to locate a website which can deliver or provide the reports on sales for your stock.

Usually, these websites will send you emails when someone downloads your inventory. If they do pay you for their purchase, they will provide you with e-mail updates and may even mail you invoices to pay for their purchases. These features are nice to have, but what's more crucial is knowing the way your inventory is performing on a specific website.

The ability to determine whether a photo will sell or not is an excellent method to alter your approach as photographer. As photographer, you must make use of this opportunity and gain insight into how your portfolio is performing.

Not just to help you grow as photographer, but also for your knowledge of the market. Based on the demand worldwide, certain kinds of stock are sold more than others. There are certain times when a particular kind of photo is popular as well as seasons when it does well but not. It is crucial that the Microstock photographer be aware of these trends to make the most of their efforts.

The websites mentioned earlier provide contributors with access to their sales reports as well as views. They are perfect for newcomers who are looking to understand the market as well as for those who are seeking an edge in the market.

Chapter 6: Create A Business Bank Account

The next step of the process to start your photography business is to start by opening a bank account for your business. It is likely to be the shortest chapter in the book since it's the most simple step of the entire procedure! This is also a signal that you're getting closer to the end of the road! The opening of a business bank account is crucial because you need an option to distinguish between both your business and personal financials. This will make keeping an eye on your finances and maximising your tax return much simpler and less complicated than having your entire financial information all swathed up in one account. Believe me when I say this makes life much simpler for all.

If you visit the bank to have your business account set-up, you'll have to talk to an individual bank representative (as as opposed to the bank teller) So you'll be required to join the waiting list and then wait in line patiently until you get your turn. My experience has shown that this waiting time can be long , depending on the number of people are waiting. I always carry a nice book or some other type of entertainment with me whenever I visit the bank. This is why it is vital to have all the documents and information you've accumulated so far in order to avoid the bank employee telling you (after all the you've been waiting) that you have to be back later, because you do not have the right details to to create your account with a bank.

The two most important requirements for creating your banking account will include your EIN as well as your company license. These two requirements could be a problem in the process of opening your company bank account, which could lead to the bank representative insisting that you return after you have the items. It is getting obvious why this book is organized in this manner, and the reason I advise you following each step to wait until you receive some kind of approval. When I spoke to my bank's representative in the local area and he thanked me for having these items in my bag. The process was extremely easy because I had all my documents in order. He also said that a lot of people are able to opening their bank accounts for business without any preparation or understanding the requirements. To sum up, minimize time and effort for everyone by being ready.

One of the steps to getting a business bank account is having to listen to bank reps' solicitations to buy additional services and products. Items such as business credit cards, credit card readers, checks and so on. These items, naturally are totally up depending on your needs. It is recommended that you take the information home and do some research prior to committing to anything in a moment. At the very least, walk out with a new , integrated business bank account as well as an application that has been approved for an enterprise debit card. When you've accomplished this step, you're now ready for your next step. Remember that you'll need to wait for a few business days before your debit card for business arrives through the post, however it shouldn't hinder you from going out and launching your the business.

Chapter 7: Making A Business Plan

Take everything you have learned from this book to date and incorporate it in the business strategy you have created. Before you write your business plan you need to determine the kind of business you run. There are a variety of types that include:

* Corporations: A separate legal entity. It's owned by shareholders as are the corporations you find on the stock market. It's highly unlikely that your business will be a corporation at first.

*Cooperatives are also known as co-ops. It's basically an organization of people that work together to profit themselves. When people are part of an organization, there usually isn't much cash because it's just an open-air space for members to work, and display their efforts.

* Partnerships are an organization that is run with two or more individuals. In the event that you own a company associate or anyone who earns a profit from the work you do, your company could be classified as to be a partnership.

* Sole traders This is a company that is run solely by you.

"Limited liability" corporations: A private limited corporation. It's similar to a mixture of either a sole proprietorship, or partnership and an organization. It's designed for smaller businesses however, it provides protection to owners of smaller businesses. This is because should the company be sued, the company's owners will not lose the entire company.

Now let's look at how to create your business plan. It is important to begin the process with your statement of mission.

Mission Statement

The mission statement of your company should be a reflection of what your company's mission statement is about. It could also be about the reasons you began taking photos in the beginning. It should also highlight the specific goals of your business. Have you got a specific goal? What type of image do you wish to convey to your clients? What kind of services do you plan to offer? It's your choice. If you can come up with an excellent goal statement for your business, then you may decide to use it for your company. It is also possible to be able to keep it as a private guideline to you.

Resume and Bio

If you haven't yet prepared your resume, take the time to do it. Keep in mind that when you write a resume that's related to photography there is no need to mention the time you worked as a secretary in an office for dental work. Make sure to include your photography achievements first. If you did acquire a valuable ability during your job as a secretary like the ability to make an excel spreadsheet, then it should be included on your list of abilities.

Additionally, you should write a personal statement. In it you (and your spouse) will write about the journey you took to become a photographer and why you love what you do in your work. Create a compelling and engaging document. I also recommend putting the two files on your site to ensure that prospective clients are confident in your abilities and passion. If you believe it's essential to print several duplicates of your resume to hand out upon request of any potential customer.

Summary of Company

This should include a description about the kind of company you manage. You can refer back to the kinds I mentioned at the beginning of this chapter. The section must also include an overview of your startup. Your startup summary should be an inventory of all assets that you have that could be used for the business. This could include equipment or furniture you have (so when you own two lights and a camera this is considered to be startup, even if you've had these for a long time) or simply funds that you must specifically invest in this business. Remember that starting a business is distinct from overhead and everything you purchase from now on needs to be reported as overhead.

In addition to what you have as a startup, it is important to keep track of the long-term assets you require as well as their estimated value. Anything you have that could be considered startup must be evaluated for value. The assessment should be conducted by a professional and then the item should be covered at the amount in the event of an accident or break-in. In the next section of the report, you'll complete a cost breakdown.

The description of business services

It's similar to the mission statements you have, but that it doesn't have to be as compelling. It's enough to describe what you intend to provide as a comprehensive description. This means you'll need to create a separate section for each product or service you intend to provide with a projected price or price ranges. It is recommended to present the price in a graph to ensure that potential customers or investors can refer to it in a short time. It should contain the cost of each service you're going to provide even if it's included in a different price. This includes pricing for photo packages, the cost to shoot, editing packaging, printing and anything other you can think of. Keep in mind that these are only estimates of costs and prices.

Client Base

This is a short overview of the customers you'd like to contact. If you've already put together an Facebook promotional campaign you can make this a reference. What are their ages? Do they belong to a certain segment? What is the average amount your typical customer earn?

External Evaluation

This means that you take a look of the business environment is similar to. Are you in a good position financially? What is the performance of similar photography studios or fine artists working in the same area? This is where the research you conducted to determine pricing competitiveness comes into play. Make sure to list precisely who your competitors are. In the event that your market saturated, you can simply write down your five most competitive competitors. You can even create charts of rates so that you can refer to it to determine an average price.

Within this area, provide the support you provide. Support services can include others you'll need to add to your team to help make your company operate efficiently. If you contract out your printing, that's one of them. If you frequently employ local makeup artists and hair stylists, make sure you list their names as well. It's recommended to note all their contact details to keep in one place. You should also include backup services to be prepared in the event that you find yourself stuck.

Planning for Marketing, Financial and Strategic Plan and Strategy

Briefly explain your marketing plan and explain how you intend to implement it. Include every method and tool you employ to help spread the word about your company, regardless of whether it's paid or free. It's also a good idea to have a financial plan. What other steps do you plan to take in order to not just ensure that your business is able to stay afloat, but also to help it grow? This is where you'll need to keep a daily record of all the spreadsheets you have, your profit as well as losses. You should also keep track of your plans for the upcoming year, and any other financial issues you might be facing.

Team

What is your current team? Yourself? Business partners? Anybody who can provide additional funding? Anyone who is a photo assistant or editors who are outsourced? Do you have makeup or hair artists? You should update it when changes happen.

Goals

Always finish your business plan using your goals in mind. Utilize a time-line of one year five years, 10 years. Be sure that your goals are realistic and achievable. Review your progress every six months to check how close you are to achieving your goal for the year.

Chapter 8: What Is Stock Photography?

In essence it is stock photography where the photographer creates an image and sells it later. This differs from the usual income model for photographers, where images could be purchased or ordered in advance. When we think of stock photography, we often consider'microstock'. Microstock is when photographers make their photos available under a royalty-free licence This implies that the user purchases an authorization to utilize the image in the way they would like. This kind of stock photography will be the main focus on this volume.

In the past, photography stock required the sale of the complete rights of ownership for an image to the purchaser[3(3). Photography stock was offered in the form of "rights handled" images that permitted the buyer to make use of the image subject to certain terms. This is the standard marketplace for photography stock, and is commonly called'macrostock'. Macrostock has become a smaller market following the introduction of microstock. It's only available to photographers who make use of high-end equipment as well as have a an established personal brand. This type of stock photography is not the subject of this article, but it is a different type of stock photography you could come across.

Other kinds of stock

Editorial

Editorial stock photography is a subset of microstock that meets the demands of media outlets. They differ from standard stock photography because they might contain distinctive logos or even people. They generally sell at a significantly greater price than regular stock photography. However, since they are designed for newspapers and websites they have smaller numbers of images that are suitable for editorial. Editorial images are also sold in much smaller amounts since they're typically only appropriate to a specific piece of news. Editorial photos are sold but not in huge numbers. They also don't have repeat sales, that makes them profitable during the brief period of time they're relevant. While they can bring in money for the photographer, it is not compatible with the passive income model.

Editorial might be a field you'd like to explore. It could be suitable if you're capable of shooting at the location of an exciting event or location[5However, this usually involves being in specific and competitive areas. Editorial requires lots of effort and time to create photos that only be sold for a brief duration; this is the result of making money from time. This is why there are many professional photographers who specialize in the field of editorial as a profession However, this need for changing time into cash and the inability to sustain sales mean that this is not a good fit for the model of passive income.

Stock footage

Stock footage is similar to stock photography with the exception it focuses on video content, not images. Once you've mastered the process of making photographs that are well-received, it is possible to move into stock footage, as it's an area that has greater earnings per download and has less competition than traditional photography that is available in stock. It is possible to wait until you're confident with stock photography before making the move to stock footage since there are various skills and equipment you'll need to master to succeed. In the beginning, you'll require camera equipment capable of creating high-quality video, as the video setting on a lot of basic DSLRs won't be sufficient to produce stock footage. Also, you will need to buy and be confident in using video editing software since stock footage requires a more extensive editing. Stock footage isn't into the guidelines of this book, but it's a fantastic supplement for passive income models and suggested as a great option to diversify your portfolio.

Stock illustration

Stock illustrations are very popular. This is a specific area of art designed for use in various commercial applications. Since the designs need an artist's help to design these designs, there is less competition as well as a larger degree of distinction. Stock illustration demands a level imagination and artistic talent that many people lack. If you are skilled in graphic design or drawing it is a field that could work for you. To make stock illustrations you'll need to utilize a different software than photographs, however with a bit of extra money this could be a great part of your portfolio of passive income.

What should you Expect from stock photography?

Photography stock is competitive market. In the beginning, just professional photographers participated in the development of stock photography, and it was definitely a market for sellers. Since then, a lot of people have joined the stock photography market and the competition is intense, anyone with a smartphone could effectively become an stock photographer (but most will not be successful). It's a good thing with the advancement of technology, the more people are requiring photographs that are stock to use in their work, and the majority of images available offered aren't of the best quality. If you are able to create high quality images , you'll beat out the majority of your competitors.

As of the date when this article was written, the largest and most well-known stock photography company is Shutterstock. Shutterstock has more than 250 million images to purchase, and has around 1.3 million images added every week. Most of the photos uploaded are not of high-quality and there's still a huge market for high-quality photographs. The good news and the bad news is that, in the 10 years since stock photography has become popular and gaining popularity, many of the images that have been uploaded remain relevant. That means that photos older than 10 years old are in the race to get new sales, however, it is also a sign that photographs that you submit are still able to be sold and earn income for the rest of time This is why stock photography such a great option as a business model that is passive in nature. Although earnings can vary from agency to agency contributors are paid approximately $0.50 per download from Shutterstock and many contributors boast an average earnings of one dollar per image for the year. So, a well-diversified portfolio of 1,200 photos is expected to yield an average that is $100 monthly. Also, you can expect to experience good but also bad years as a contributor to stock In some instances, this could be due to the fact that certain photos are seasonal (such for Christmas pictures) or it could be due to luck. In the same way, certain areas of photography have a longer shelf lives than others[6[6].

A Experiment: 10 years as an photographer for stock

This book is designed to demonstrate the ways stock photography can create an effective passive income stream. As we've mentioned the majority of contributors be in agreement that an average of one image each year is a realistic amount for a stock photographer.

It's not expected to quit your job to become a stock photographer, however the idea of contributing 100 photos each month to your portfolio of stock images can be achieved with any schedule.

The first two years

Based on this model, if we consider that your stock portfolio will generate one image every year, and you add 100 images each month to your portfolio of stocks and you expect to build a portfolio that increases with every passing month. By the close of the second year, you'll have a portfolio consisting of 2,400 imagesand earning $200 per month in the average. Based on this approach then, you can anticipate your income cumulative over the first two years to be as follows:

The initial 24 month of earnings would be similar to the following:

Month	Portfolio size	Revenue	Cumulative income
1	100	$ 8.33	$ 8
2	200	$ 16.67	$ 25
3	300	$ 25.00	$ 50
4	400	$ 33.33	$ 83
5	500	$ 41.67	$ 125
6	600	$ 50.00	$ 175
7	700	$ 58.33	$ 233
8	800	$ 66.67	$ 300
9	900	$ 75.00	$ 375
10	1000	$ 83.33	$ 458
11	1100	$ 91.67	$ 550
12	1200	$ 100.00	$ 650
13	1300	$ 108.33	$ 758
14	1400	$ 116.67	$ 875
15	1500	$ 125.00	$ 1,000
16	1600	$ 133.33	$ 1,133
17	1700	$ 141.67	$ 1,275
18	1800	$ 150.00	$ 1,425
19	1900	$ 158.33	$ 1,583
20	2000	$ 166.67	$ 1,750
21	2100	$ 175.00	$ 1,925
22	2200	$ 183.33	$ 2,108
23	2300	$ 191.67	$ 2,300
24	2400	$ 200.00	$ 2,500

If you decide after two years that you decided not to create any more photos to be used in stock photography, you'd have already earned $2,500 in extra income during those initial two years. However, the best part with an income stream that is passive is the fact that the portfolio will continue to earn income even when you do not actively contribute. Even if you haven't created stock photography after the initial 2 years, at the fifth year's end, you'd earned $9,700.

In the first 10 years

Let's keep this as an example and suppose that you don't wish to invest in your portfolio of stocks after the initial two years. The portfolio will continue to bring in income in the following 10 years, and you'd have accumulated the sum of $21,700. This is all for creating 100 images every month for two years.

If you'd been producing 100 images per month for the entire 10 years [7], you'd have an archive of 12,000 photos each month that produced $1,000 and earning a total of $60,500 during that time. This is an average of $504 per month over 10 years [88.

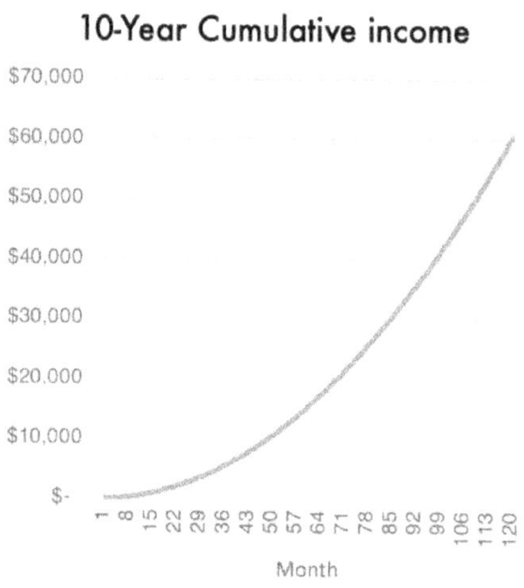

It is evident that, the majority of the earnings generated are earned later. In this example, if the photographer creates 100 photos per month, less than $15,000 will be produced over the first five years, however, more than $45,000 over the course of five years.

Stock photography is a lucrative business in the long run, but it isn't going to turn you into a millionaire and you can't anticipate to earn money in a matter of days (this is an issue for those who are new contributors as it could take months before you get the first sales). It may take a long period of time for quality photos to gain prominence in images searches, as the most popular ones rise in results. It also takes an extended period of time to discover the types of images that sell for you. This is often a long period of effort and time. It should be your aim not to create great images, instead of creating images that will be well-sellers over time.

Stock photography is an excellent opportunity to earn passive income if you're passionate about and have a photography. I'm sure you have, otherwise you wouldn't have read this book. If you are a fan of the creative process associated with photography , then the effort it requires will not be as if it's work and you'll be earning long-term income from your passion. Many people are looking for passive income as they do not like the routine of a nine-to-five job This may be the case for you additional income sources can provide you with a better assurance of financial security in the event that you need to quit your job. If you're looking to step back from your current position stock photography can offer you additional security and skills that you require to join the world of photography and be the boss of your life.

How can I start with stock photography? Photography is a field that is both technical and artistic. This requires equipment as well as the right capabilities and skills to get the most out of your photos. In this section , we'll discuss what is required for photographers to to not only be a part of the market of stock photography and produce photos that can compete effectively in the market. Although not all the equipment listed in this article is essential for all photographers, some tools will be specific and will aid you in entering areas of photography with less competition , and a higher earnings potential.

If you're a novice to stock photography, it might appear as if there's an abundance of equipment required to get into the market for photography however, this isn't accurate. The minimum requirement is a camera that is decent as well as a basic editing software[99. One way to reduce the expense of purchasing the latest equipment is to invest your profits in new equipment. It can reduce your income early and could mean that you enter other markets later on, but it's a great way to master the use of your equipment piece by piece one time, and also to ensure that your company is earning you money and not putting you in a position to spend cash.

Equipment
Camera

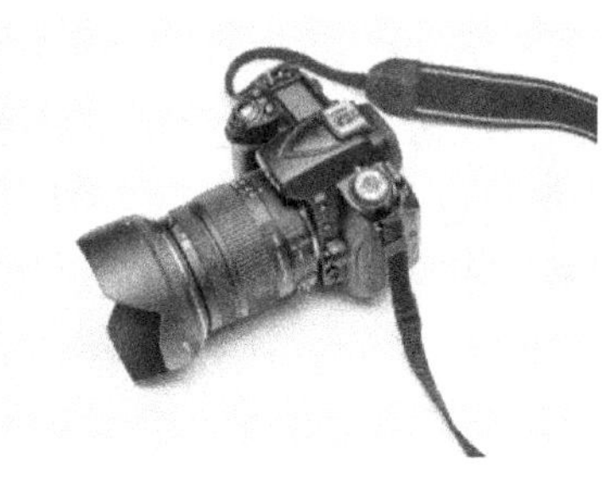

Your DSLR is going to be your new greatest friend.

The camera is the sole piece of equipment is essential to begin creating profitable stock photography. There is no need for cameras to be brand new There are a variety of old and used cameras available at reasonable prices and are suitable for stock photography. In general that is the case, all professional cameras manufactured within the last five years will suffice to use for stock photography. Although cheaper cameras can be used as stock cameras, the more expensive cameras offer higher resolution, greater overall image quality, and better overall control of the photo but these benefits are merely bonuses and not essential. For a camera that is entry-level the most important thing is that your camera can be used with interchangeable lenses and at a minimum 12 megapixels.

If you are buying a camera, you might want to consider the cost of buying the body (a camera that does not have lens) and then buying the lens separately. This gives you more control over the setup of your camera and can save money in the event that you intend for a lens upgrade later on.

With advances in technology for smartphones, you might be tempted to utilize its camera to capture your photos initially. It is not advised, because you will be unable to control the image's quality. you can exercise over your photo is not the same as the ones images that sell well through stock agencies. The primary issue is the size of the sensors and lenses that, although acceptable for photography for the casual photographer, it will not be suitable for stock photos. Some agencies use programs to recognize photos captured using smartphones. And even if your images are approved as stock, they won't be able to compete with others captured with a high-quality camera.

DSLR Or mirrorless?

There are pros and cons to both kinds of cameras However, in general, mirrorless cameras are likely to be more expensive and lower quality end on the scale. Mirrorless cameras don't have many of the internal components included in DSLRs, which makes them less efficient and more expensive. DSLR that makes them less expensive and lighter than the DSLR equivalent. Mirrorless cameras cannot permit you to view the through directly from their lens which can make it difficult to determine the quality of the image particularly in low-light conditions. The most effective cameras you can purchase are DSLRs. However, you'll need a basic camera in order for stock photography and buying a new mirrorless camera has substantial cost savings.

Lenses

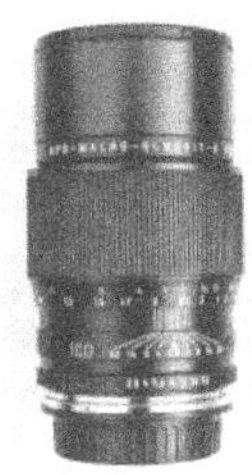

Quality of photographs will be influenced by the lens that is used. Lenses can be useful for many different reasons and enable photographers to be able to respond to different conditions and situations. When you reach the point at which you want to purchase additional lenses, then it's advised to invest in top quality lenses. Lenses aren't affected by being out of date just like cameras as the technology they are based upon is generally constant, which means that the lens that is good, taken care of, is likely to last longer than the camera it was purchased for.

When purchasing lenses, it is recommended to avoid purchasing lens

kits, or that you upgrade the lens you have purchased as quickly as you can. Kit lenses are those that are typically included with the DSLR. Although they can be effective but their quality may limit a photographer. It is usually the 18-55mm lenses included on the DSLR and are made with less durable and low-quality materials.
Macro lens

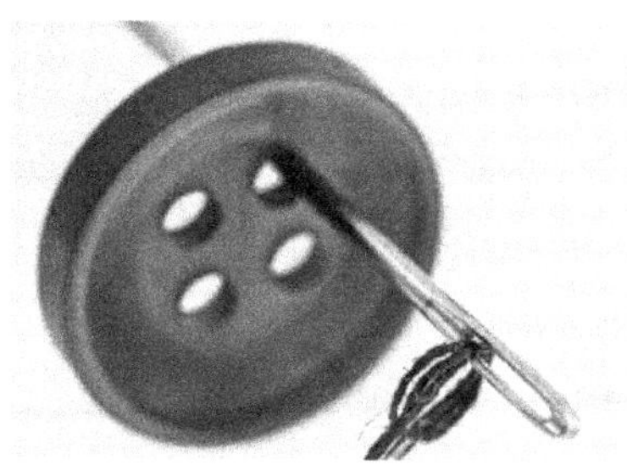

Even though they're highly specialized close-up shots such as this are not possible with standard kit lenses. They require an extra macro lens.

A standard kit lens should be able to focus an object that is at least 25cm of the lens. In order to capture photographs in which the subject is closer and magnified using a macro lens, it is needed. Macro lenses allow photographers to concentrate on tiny subjects or subjects that normally are too close for photography in the way they are intended. The use of macro lenses can greatly increase the possibilities of photographer, and should be considered after you've started to see increases in sales for your portfolio.

Macro lenses are helpful to:

* Flowers
* Jewellery
* Nature and insects
* Mechanical components

Telephoto lens

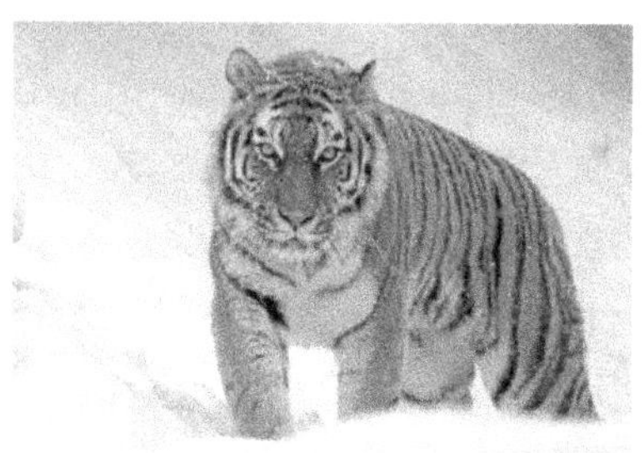

It's not always advisable to reach out to your subject in order to take photos of it. Telephoto lenses are the reverse of macro lenses. That is, they can be useful in photography of subjects that are distant. Telephoto lenses are those large lenses you've been able to see being employed by professional photographers during games and on documentaries on wildlife as an excellent zoom lens can be used to capture a subject at far away, in situations where it isn't suitable to take a photo of close to it[1010.

Telephoto lenses don't necessarily require you to focus on a particular subject from the distance, but could be beneficial when taking cities or landscapes. The special feature of telephoto lenses is that distances between objects that are further or closer to the camera appear less, creating an overall look that is more flatter. Even at close distances this feature can be utilized to create more accurate (and more attractive) photos of individuals.

Telephoto lenses are helpful to:

* Sport
* Wildlife
* Portraiture
* Cityscapes

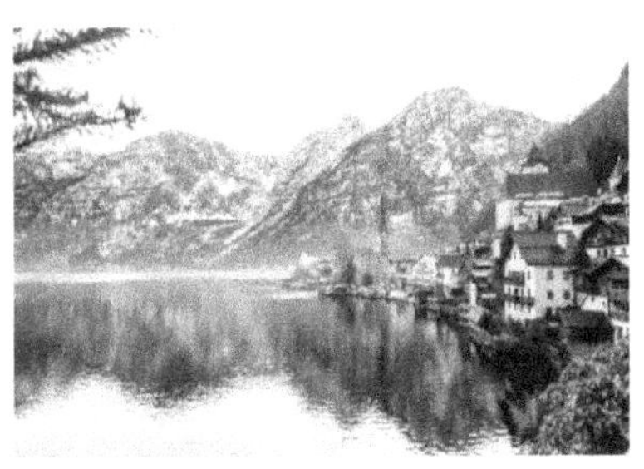

Wide-angle lens

Wide-angle lenses allow photographers more freedom when framing their image. This lens lets photographers create a larger image from the same place. This increases the distance between the objects in the foreground and background. Wide-angle lenses do exactly that, they can capture the image from the wide angle. It can be difficult to determine whether an image was taken using wide-angle lenses but it's an instrument that offers the photographer greater flexibility. By using a wide-angle lens the photographer can take more photos from one spot (without having to go back). Wide-angle lenses also possess the capability of increasing their distances between objects closer or farther away from the camera.

Chapter 9: Succeeding With Landscape Photography

Great landscape photography sells because the buyer is seeking the desire to imagine and escape. We as a species have always been drawn with and drawn by the natural world. If you're nature, away from noise, what do you notice? Do you sense the appeal and feel the attraction?

To create a stunning landscape, you must be aware of the landscape and the way light affects it. You must have a passion for the earth and an intimate connection to the natural world.

The best way of doing this is to check out a place on your own by foot before taking photos. While doing this, look for:

"Light" (highlights as well as shadows).

color (discord as well as harmony).

Shapes (angular and circular).

Composition (weak and strong).

the texture (smooth as well as rough).

patterns (odd or even).

Tone (dark as well as light).

If, for example, next moment you're out with your camera looking for that wide-open view of rolling hills and mountains Also, take note of the specific particulars of the landscape, and maybe just snap a small portion of the overall image.

Your personal vision and style should be evident in every photo you shoot It's your responsibility to capture the essence of the scene before you. If your image is good for the viewer, the person viewing your photo will feel like they are in your picture and feel the sensation that they are there. A stunning landscape photo can be a wonderful escape.

Creating Great Outdoor Portraits

If you've taken pictures of an escape to the countryside, family reunion, or a unique holiday getaway with your friends or family members you know that outdoor photography may present different challenges. This is true even for the best professional photographer.

Direct sunlight could be harsh. Unwanted things could disrupt your composition. A proper color rendering may cause problems. Sometimes the environment isn't being cooperative.

There's nothing that can be done to improve the natural world However, with persistence and practice, you'll be able to overcome a number of other issues you face as a photographer who shoots outdoors. In my time as photographer, I've discovered a variety of ways to shoot outdoors that can benefit those who are in need.

Don't get confused

When you're creating your image, you want to make your object the focal point that all viewers are drawn to. Large areas, hectic patterns with vibrant colors (specifically the mix of different shades) or overly imposing patterns within your backgrounds or in your foreground that aren't dealt with in a proper manner could be a distraction if you're not mindful.

Take Control Of the Depth Of Field

Mountains that are in the distance or the edges of a forest can create a beautiful background for your goal provided you can control the field of view. If you're using an SLR camera, you could adjust your depth of field to make the background completely away from your intended target.

This serves as a control of the eyes for the person viewing your photo. The eyes are usually drawn to the most bright part of the picture. If your subject is highly concentrated in relation with the background your object will get highlighted and become the focal point of your photo. Controlling the depth of field can be achieved by calibrating the aperture setting.

The smaller the f-stop and the greater the opening to your camera, as well as the smaller your depth-of-field likely to be. For instance, if you look at a photograph in a nature magazine of stunning butterflies within an area of flowers and the butterfly is in sharp focus, but the flowers are blurred. This was accomplished by a professional photographer using an extremely narrow distance of focus.

In bright lighting conditions this may be difficult to achieve. For any intensity of light when you increase your aperture (lower the f-stop) you will need to increase the speed of shutter (thus decreasing the direct exposure time) to avoid overexposure. The speed you increase the shutter usually reduces the resolution of the image. Find the right combination of aperture and shutter speed setting that gives you the result you desire.

Beware of distracting items behind your target.

What's clearly an ordinary mailbox, bush, or even a birdhouse for your eyes, may appear as an extra extension of the top of the head of your target in the 2D image. It is possible to achieve some interesting outcomes by doing this but they won't impress your subject. Take the time to identify the most intriguing angle to get rid of any disruptive elements from the background.

Take control of the unwanted light

Due to the patterns of shadows it creates Certain types of light are able to bring out the worst of the target. Lateral light is the type you ought to choose. Lateral light can be controlled and directed to create stunning shadow patterns across the area of your goal. There's a saying that applies to numerous professionals who photograph outdoors, "the initial tree in the forest is best" to create an ideal background.

The explanation isthat your canopy from the first tree is responsible for the strong downlight, but since it is on the edge to the woods, you have light from the lateral side to deal with. Similar principles apply to patios, or the edges of any other overhang.

Professional photographers who are skilled often use reflectors and shade cloths to block light while directing the light that is available to enhance their goals and get the desired result.

Change The Color

Prior to the age of digital the corrective filtering or specially-made films were mostly used to correct color in photographs taken outside. Digital cameras allow you can fix the color through the use of the white balance settings. Many digital cameras nowadays do a good job of instantly altering the white balance to match exterior exposures.

Making sure your composition is simple by controlling your depth of field and removing items that could distract away from your goal and help to highlight your subject as the main focus of your photo. Controlling the natural light that is available and adjusting the white balance of your photographs will help to expose and enhance the real attraction of your object.

Beyond that Make it your aim each all day long to let your mind run wild so that you can be able to see things around you unique and new ways. Never be content with being able to see the common as normal.

The art of creating art is created by people who are able to look beyond the usual and to think about their environment in a unique way and to demonstrate their understanding to other people. Thus, be adventurous and don't be afraid to try something new.

The world is abundant in shapes and colors, textures in patterns, patterns, and forms of light. Magnificent man-made structures and stunning landscapes aren't necessary to create stunning images outdoors.

Chapter 10: Getting The Basics

Find a photography class

You must definitely consider investing into a photography class or workshop. But, don't go for the first option you find. Instead, conduct some thorough investigation first. Things to consider before taking a photography class are as follows:

• Who will be the teacher?

* Are they famous experts?

* What is the course plans and schedule?

* Who were some of those who have been students in the course?

* Does the way of teaching match your interests and needs?

When you review all of these aspects, you'll be able to determine the courses that are worth your time and money and which could benefit you. Whatever the case it's likely to go without that you select only courses taught by experts in their fields.

Knowing the basics of the camera inside and out is an absolute requirement. Cameras today have a variety of options to use for specific scenarios, but If you're not aware of how to compose or expose properly and properly, there's no way to do well in this regard. It is also important knowing your camera since when you are in a photography session, you'll have to locate and utilize the buttons to adjust the shutter speed, ISO and aperture adjustments without removing your eyes off the viewfinder. If you are able to master the use of all these, then you need to begin thinking about taking an editing course for photography.

Find an instructor

Another method of learning is to find a great mentor. The mentor you choose should someone who has a career that is successful, that you admire as well as someone who's passionate about the work she/he does. When you have found an ideal mentor, you should be able to analyze his/her work, look for sources of inspiration, and then design your own photographs.

It is recommended to submit your photographs to your instructor and they will give you feedback and suggestions regarding how you can make your photos better. There is a chance that some photos you consider to be your top ones aren't getting the reviews or comments you expected. Don't be dissatisfied and be grateful for every piece of advice you receive from your coach.

The reason this happens is because you're too focused on your work, and it can be difficult to step back from the work you do and assess your photographs objectively. This is precisely why you require an expert who can be able to objectively examine your photos and analyze them, then suggest modifications.

Take advantage of constructive critique

If you are a student or not, you must learn to accept different comments and take advantage of constructive criticism. This is the way through which you'll gain the most. Sharing your pictures with your friends and family members is good and you can be sure that they will always be impressed and stunned by your photographs.

If you only listen on their praises, then you'll quickly begin to believe you've already got everything and you'll never make progress. Instead, you should show your photographs to professionals you see across and be open to their critique.

Learn while you are at home

There will be an time, especially when you're at the beginning of your journey, where you'll have none clients at all. Even if you do have regular work , but you have an hour or two of free time, you should use the time in a wise way. You could, for instance, create your own personal goals and conduct shoots that is inspiring to you or perhaps something is not something that you could really identify with and your personal style. This manner, you'll experiment with and test out new designs lens, locations and ideas.

Shoot in RAW

Always shoot always in RAW. Shooting in RAW means that the file you download to your computer holds all of the original data the camera has taken. Another popular format used is JPEG but it's an uncompressed file format which means it only retains approximately half the information in the file. So, if you'd like to be sure not to be shocked by how different the photos will appear when you upload onto your personal computer it is recommended to shoot RAW format.

Learn how to shoot manual mode.

It is suggested to begin learning to shoot in manual mode as you'll have a better knowledge about your camera and the lighting around you, and how you can make use of this light to create amazing images. If you start by learning this it will help you enhance your photography later as well as your ability.

If you are relying on specific modes of shooting that you use in specific circumstances and you don't have an understanding of all that is happening with your camera. You will never be able with the settings to create some unique photographs. Manual mode lets you remain more consistent in your exposure, which in turn helps you save time when editing.

Get inspired and design your own style

Don't be fooled into thinking that you'll get ideas exclusively by looking at photographers' work and the works of other artists. If you do that you'll create photographs that look similar to those that you see on a regular basis and all you'll need is to be different. Instead of copying and replicating the style of other photographers You can find inspiration virtually anywhere including comic books, movies and paintings dancing, plays and so on.

It's normal to think that you might feel comfortable to shoot the same way as other shooters do because it seems right, reliable and secure. But, it won't attract clients or will be able to establish that profitable business you've been dreaming of. You must offer something that is unique to your customers You must look outside of the norm if would like to stand out and develop your own style that is reflective of your personality and the way you feel about photography.

Choose your specialization

Once you are in the point of making great photographs, it is important to consider the photography genres that best suit your tastes as well as your attitudes and passions. There are many different fields and topics, like street photography, food photography fashion, automobile weddings family, baby landscape, black and white and portrait photography, and more. Pick what you like and keep learning, exploring and taking practice.

You shouldn't be obligated to perform only one type of photography. For instance, you could you can do wedding and baby photography or wedding, baby or portrait photos. The possibilities are endless. However, why is it necessary to narrow your focus to only one or two areas of photography?

The answer is straightforward. As a highly demanding discipline photography requires a lot of capabilities, so it's best to focus on only a handful of fields and strive to be the best at these than to waste your efforts on all the photography styles that are possible that are available, and there are many.

Create a group of friends who you trust

If your business is growing and you are now required to collaborate with other artists too including makeup or hair stylists It is likely that you will require some time to identify the ones that complement your style of shooting. It is essential to choose those you can collaborate with as an untrained hair stylist or makeup artist can ruin the entire shoot.

How to Market Yourself

Create your portfolio

Making your portfolio is essential. How can you draw clients in when you don't have examples of photos to showcase? Your portfolio should contain the best images that represent your expertise, style and what you excel at. When you are creating your portfolio, keep in your mind that simplicity is most important factor, since your portfolio shouldn't appear overwhelming to your customers.

Therefore, make it as simple as possible but arrange it in a way that, with only a few photographs you are able to easily differentiate yourself, showcase your work and draw customers. If you're brand new at this and encounter difficulties to create your portfolio and want to avoid that step completely, you shouldn't think about it. Making a portfolio can be time-consuming particularly when you're just beginning your journey.

If you're still slightly confused because you don't know you like and aren't sure what style will best fit you, you could consider taking photos at no cost, examining the styles you love and you'll have some fantastic images for your portfolio.

If you have created your portfolio, it's not a guarantee that, once you've created it, you don't have to take any action on it for a while. In fact, your it is necessary to edit your portfolio regularly.

Create your own website

When you are creating your website, you should consider hiring a professional to create it for you, as your website must be attractive. It is recommended to have the photos on your site divided into categories, so it appears more well-organized. Include a picture of yourself along with some details about yourself and your experiences.

If you are able, include a portion of your pricing and, more importantly, provide your contact details. Your website's design will also reveal who your customers are. For instance, if you specialize in wedding photos, then your site must be designed in so as to draw the clients who require this type of service.

Once you've set up your site Don't wait for people to see it. In reality, people aren't interested in what you're doing. You must instead get them to care. Therefore, creating your brand, logo, and website is only the beginning. Now you must go out and promote your business and yourself and let people know about your offerings.

Promote your work

It is important to realize that creating great images isn't the only thing essential to begin your company. Marketing tactics could include using social media, attending local events, referring to others and word of mouth, internet advertising, etc.

When you consider marketing, keep in mind that you must think about your customers and not your own needs. Therefore, you should think about what your clients require and the type of relationship you would like to build with them. Additionally, the first impressions of your customers are crucial. Therefore, you should be aware of this when you design the content for your business.

Referrals are vital to the growth of your company. You must work hard to earn them, but you can also encourage them. For example, you can offer your customers the stack of business cards and their pictures to distribute to their family and friends.

You can gather email addresses and attempt to advertise your business and draw customers through this approach in addition to mailing them a monthly newsletter. Be sure to use social media and let people know about your company.

You could also join forces with charities, as an example since the people who are wealthy and attend these events will learn about your business and what you do which means that you might meet potential clients.

Chapter 11: Understanding Exposure

If you're the first person to start trying to comprehend digital photography it may seem so difficult that you believe you'll not be able to succeed. However, in this book you're going to be taught everything you must be aware of about digital photography.

The first thing to know is about exposure. There is an exposure triangle. It comprises: shutter speed, aperture, and ISO. In lieu of getting technical about these I'll dissect it in order so that you can understand what they are.

Many people love to employ metaphors in explaining the triangle of exposure, which is exactly my goal. If your camera is like a window. Your the aperture will depend on the size of the window. When you have a narrow window, only a tiny amount of light is allowed to pass through However, if you have a bigger window it will allow more light to enter.

It is similar to shutters on windows, if you shut them swiftly the light is not able to enter the space than if you closed them slowly. Imagine that you're in the space that has a window and you're wearing sunglasses. The longer you wear the glasses on, the less sunlight reflects on your. This is similar to having the low ISO.

In this room, there are three ways to enhance your exposure to light. It is possible to leave the shutters in place for an extended duration of time. This is similar to slowing down the shutter speed of your camera. You can also increase your window size. This could mean increasing the aperture of your camera. You can also remove your sunglasses, which is a way of making the ISO setting bigger.

This might not be the ideal scenario, but I'm sure that you can see the image. Imagine that you take off your sunglasses, and then increase the size of the window. you might find that this permits too much light into the glass. You might think that the solution to rectify this issue is to reduce your window's size however, when you do that you will not get enough light to allow you to open the shutter for a longer period of time.

Do you get the message I'm trying to convey? It is true that I can't give you exact guidelines on what settings to make in terms of aperture, ISO, or shutter speed, because it all depends on the surrounding conditions and level of lighting.

Remember that when changing an aperture's aperture ISO and shutter speed it will alter the aspects of the exposure too. If, for instance, you alter the aperture you also alter the depth of field. If you alter the shutter speed, you're changing the way that motion is captured. Likewise, by changing the ISO you're changing how grainy the image is captured.

One of the best advantages of Digital cameras is the fact that they can experiment with different settings and see what one suits your specific requirements most. Furthermore, you can observe the results right away. It isn't necessary to wait for film be developed in order to determine whether you have the right setting.

Another advantage is that you can select semi-manual mode. It means that you be able to control just one or two settings, and the camera will alter the rest for you. If you're still learning about digital photography, I would suggest that you try this semi-manual setting and test only 1 setting at.

ISO The lower the setting the lower the settings, the less sensitive your camera will be to light. The higher ISO settings are usually utilized in dark environments however, it is important to be aware that the higher the ISO setting, the more grainy the image will appear.

The majority of people opt to set their camera to auto mode for ISO because it will pick the lowest setting that is appropriate for the picture you're making. However, if you change the ISO setting of your camera, it can affect the shutter speed, as well as the aperture settings on your camera.

In deciding which ISO setting to choose it is important to consider whether the subject is well lit or if you prefer grainy photos or ones that is quiet, if you use a tripod, and if the photographer is standing.

If there is ample lighting and the subject isn't moving, you need an image that is quiet. If you're using a tripod, you'll choose a lower ISO setting. However when the scene is dark, and you do not mind a grainy image and you're not using the tripod and the subject is moving, you might want to raise to the ISO setting.

Aperture simply means that aperture is the measurement of the opening in the lens of your camera. The way it works is that the greater the aperture, greater amount of light passes through. The less light is able to enter through smaller openings. It is important to keep in mind when it comes to aperture is that smaller the aperture, the bigger the opening.

Depth of Field refers to the portion of your image that is in focus. Also that if you have a huge depth field, most of your photo will be focused, however when you have a smaller depth field, only the part that is close to your camera is focused.

The aperture greatly affects the your depth of field. If you opt for a wide aperture, the fields depth will diminish, and if you choose to use smaller apertures, the depth of field will grow. It can be difficult to remember. If you remember that smaller numbers result in only a tiny depth of field while large numbers can cause you to have the largest depth of field, you'll be fine.

Naturally, some photos need the use of a smaller depth field. For instance, if you're taking photos of flowers and you do not want your background focussed, this is the place you'll need a wide aperture.

Shutter Speed is the duration that the shutter remains open while taking a picture. The speed of shutters is calculated in fractions second, and the higher the lowest number of this fraction (denominator) the quicker shutter speed will be when it closes. If the shutter speed is lower than 1/60, it is necessary to utilize a tripod or otherwise you'll get the phenomenon known as camera shake . It is essentially a blurred image due to motion while you are using the shutter.

In deciding which shutter speed to select, it is important be aware of whether the object that you're trying to capture is moving and whether you wish to stop it from moving or let the movement appear in the photograph. To capture the image exactly in its entirety, you should select the fastest shutter speed however, if you wish to blur the movement you should choose slow shutter speeds.

Remember when we close this chapter that focusing on only one of the elements is not going to give you the attention you're seeking. When you make changes to one element one element, the other needs to be altered in order to create an equilibrium. It's essential to work using these three elements to discover what works best for you.

Chapter 12: Markets For Your Photographs

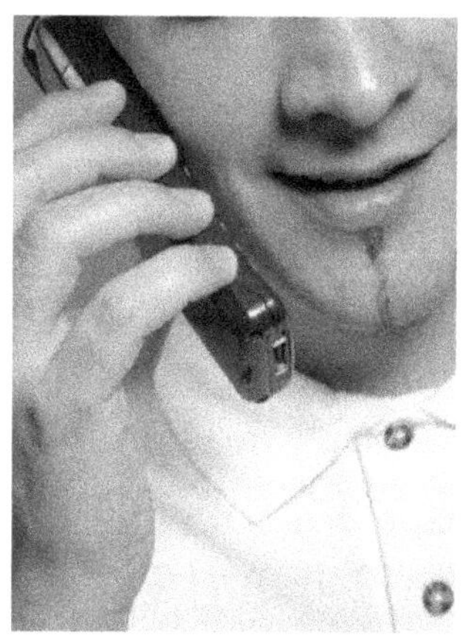

Marketing Strategies for Photographers Marketing strategies may sound like in a way, it's that you will have more money in your pockets. It is the business aspect of transferring a product an owner to another. That is, you create more sales. It's never been simpler for photographers to implement effective strategies to increase sales. Photographers are selling more that ever, yet it is also true that the marketplace has grown exponentially, and it's economically wise to take advantage of this growth.

While there are a variety of effective ways to take action but they all have national, international as well as local impacts. Certain will have an immediate impact, while others provide long-term benefits.

Local Impact Immediately.

It is not necessary to hold a doctorate in photography to figure out that the region, which is fifty miles from where you live is the one that you're familiar with the best. Expanding your horizons in the immediate vicinity can have a direct impact.

Your Marketing Strategy

Many will claim, "Hey, I'm creative! I don't require this," "****!" however, everyone requires an effective business plan in the contemporary world. It's the course you take to get started. It explains the current situation and where you're supposed to go, as well giving you the steps you need to take to meet your personal goals.

Find the place you would like to take advantage of. To ensure you stay on the right track, you must always record it in a notebook. It might seem time-consuming in the sense that it actually is however, it's an important document you can revisit frequently to see if you're meeting your personal goals. Everyone else will never read this document, however it is essential that you can discern what your weaknesses and strengths are. Otherwise, you're bound to not succeed! It might be simpler to establish the wedding photography business at your home city of Vatican City!

The outline of a marketing strategy.
Market research.
What do your customers think of your service? When you hand over your final product, you should include a pre-printed questionnaire. It is by far the best method of marketing, but it does not need to be a positive one. If no one is employing you for the second time due to an error that you committed the previous time around, then you must be aware about it in order to take corrective actions.

As with all businesses like any other, photography also is not without repeat orders. If you've photographed an event well it is possible that they will not choose you to be their photographer for the honeymoon however, your name might be remembered later in the event that "official" photos are required to commemorate the birth of the first baby, or for the christening of a child. If you're not receiving the majority from repeat customers, then why is it that you aren't getting it?

It is impossible to fix the issue without identifying the issue. This will expose your competitors' strengths, and you have to be aware of how powerful they are. Are there weaknesses that you could exploit through a price cut, or by going that extra mile for services. You must know the exact position you are within your local workforce, as well as in the context of your competitors.

Unique marketing points

What makes your business distinctive? These are the key points that you should be able to communicate when conducting target marketing. When you've been commissioned to take photos, are you willing to send a free photo enlarged, preferably onethat"tugs in the deepest part of your heart" because the subject matter is emotional? Are you willing to go the extra mile when the customer's service is involved? If you surpass your customers' expectations each time you do your job you will earn regular business. Repeat business is the foundation to success. Inattention to detail, or sloppy work to the smallest of details, will always result in unsatisfactory results. If you offer your services to individuals in any kind of "people photograph" Are you willing to scan and repair a damaged or damaged old photograph? You could even offer a fee.

Are you willing to offer the customer a no-cost compact disc with their photos on it? Exploit potential.

Many people own cameras and pets. But, it's difficult for an average person to get an image professionally with their dog! Sometimes, people love their pets more than humans. Animals always have an emotional draw. Therefore, you should get a picture of a pet The more adorable, more adorable, then then have it printed on an t-shirt, or coffee mug. Visit the local park close to where you live and wear this t-shirt. There's no need for your pet - just the camera! Request a shirt to be made for those who admire the tshirt (after taking the picture).

Print some business cards and to cover local sporting events and contests. There's always someone who doesn't have cameras who would like to take a picture with the team that won. You might also think about joining a local club and promoting your services as a photographer. There's nothing as powerful than word-of-mouth advertising.

Competition

Find out what exactly your competition is doing and what services do they offer. Send them an email, or call and request to be a prospective client. If you've received the email address, you've got a backup copy to use for reference in the future.

Also, you should check the prices regularly and update your details. It is important to be aware of how many competitions there are and if the pricing you have set is one that is competitive. Other factors to consider include such as the after-sales service for customers as well as their promotional services.

Identify your target audience.

By carefulanalysisofyourcompetitors'strengthsandweaknesses,you maybeableto find a gap in the market that you can easily tap into. If you're not able to evaluate this information yourself, consult someone who is!

Primary customers

If you are a specialist with wedding photographs, your main target is recently engaged couples. Are you consuming the advertisements for engagement in the local paper? Do you have the ability to persuade an expert in the area to put advertisements for your service within his store?

Define your short medium, long-term and short-term goals.

Are you required to attract new clients? Do you have the capacity to handle the additional demands on your time and not let your existing customers be affected? Are you seeking more clients for existing photos. What are the best places for your business to grow? Sometimes, it's necessary to be extremely ruthless in this area. "I would like to become millionaire in the blink of an eye" won't work! It is essential to set specific and realistic goals. Without this, your marketing plan will be unsuccessful. You must be able to determine if the actions you're taking are generating the outcomes you want. If you're looking to make the most profit you should try to achieve an increase around 3 percent during the course of a year rather than claim that I'm looking to triple my profits.

Profit objectives define the amount of profit that you wish the marketing effort to make. It is possible to set a goal to earn 2 percent in profit in the initial year and then increasing it by 10 percent each year after that. Do you just want to have to gain a greater share of the market in which you are operating? If so what is the best way to you find your ideal customers to make them aware of the products and services you provide?

Strategies

This is the main element of your strategy that you've identified where improvement can be made and it is crucial to take advantage of the market tools. What are you planning to do to draw new customers into purchasing your products or services? While this is possible at a national scale however, the most immediate impact is locally. It is possible to improve your business relationships by improving your skills in PR. If you've realized there's a gap on the market, then you can market and target the exact target market. It can be done through direct mail. One example is when you're an event photographer, look through the columns about engagements in the local newspapers. They're usually very specific, like "Mr R. W. Smith would like to make an announcement". There could be a number of Smiths in the directory of telephone numbers but they need to be easily traceable. Another suggestion is to study the banns of future marriages. These will provide you with an ideal clientele that you can direct mail or call directly. Contact your local church officials if they are willing to hand out some the business cards you have created. You must decide on how much time and cash you're willing to commit to this project, and establish an amount of time. It is important to determine after three or four weeks if this method is effective.

If you plan to promote in the media, you must be aware of publications and the price of the advertisement, and the length of time that advertisements will be running. Local newspapers may offer reduced rates for a lengthy running advertisements. Similar reasoning applies if you plan to use radio ads.

A timetable allows you to follow up on any leads in your business. A massive marketing campaign could be detrimental when you don't have the time to follow-up on every inquiry. Be sure to consider the other costs that may arise in connection with this campaign, like postage costs, as well as any additional printing expenses. In this time frame, you need be sure that the printing will be completed within the timeframe you've allocated. If you're unable to follow up on any leads you have generated, then do not make those leads in the first instance.

It's always more costly to attract new customers than to retain existing ones since there are always expenses. This may mean hiring an additional staff member. After reviewing the budget for an ad-hoc campaign, that this strategy isn't in your needs. It may be more beneficial to broaden your reach of sales.

Additional Ways to Broaden Your Internet Locally

Passive advertising

It is local advertising on local radio and also in the media. It might work for some but for others it's not a reliable method to generate new revenue since in certain areas the costs are prohibitive. Do not underestimate the places which offer free advertising spaces, such as supermarket billboards as well as other companies like the local developer's. This kind of passive marketing implies that the method is more effective when it's ongoing, which increases the cost. Recent research in marketing has indicated that it can be best utilized in conjunction in conjunction with other services that utilize your time and not money to ensure that you are prominent in the eyes of the public.

Put yourself visible
Enhance your profile
Are there new restaurants open near you, or is one which is being renovated? If so, inquire whether you could provide free decoration. Photographs and frame the photos, then ensure you include your contact details and your name inside the frame. While you're there try to convince them that you use the photos for their menus and cocktail menu, or even use the

cocktails to create a decor. Nothing tastes better than having a drink in front of you using the proper lighting.

Run local seminars.

Organise a local seminar no cost, and then ask your local paper to report on the event. Maybe, you can take the kids at your local school on a field trip with a camera. You may not be able to be a success however, since children are emotive subjects they will have their work presented. There is the added advantage of being praised as the person who arranged the event. There is also the possibility of receiving commissions from this.

You could always organize an adult-only seminar at no cost and even if you don't have an office. You can also check whether a church in your area will give their space away or even an existing college, school or.

Charges for field trips

If you're known and respected within your local area and have a good reputation, you might think about charging people to go out for an excursion. The idea is built for those who are sociable because the reason for the interest could be as significant as it is in your job. Be aware of any additional insurance charges you'll require in this case.

Contact your local newspaper

It is worth checking whether your local newspaper is interested in an ongoing series of stories on photography in your local area. They might even offer you a fee for this particular series, since they're always looking for content relevant to the local area. If you don't feel you're competent enough to handle this, ask your radio stations in the area whether you are able to give talks on a specific photography topic or about photography in your local area.

Make use of your website to promote your business tool

If you own a website site, you should make the most of it. Start a forum for local discussions, or give a few pages to an amateur team so that they could utilize the site as a bulletin board. The possibilities are endless here. Concentrate on the things that would be beneficial to your community and also generate publicity.

If you don't have a website you can create one free using Yahoo or Wordpress. If you don't know how to make one, then you should consider using the services of Upwork, Fiverr and Freelancer. Find people across the globe to make one for you using these websites. They will provide you with an estimate and you decide on who to pay commission. The initial cost is minimal and the cost of maintaining your website will decrease over time. A website that is yours indicates that you're dedicated to the profession of being photographer.

If you're really smart you can dedicate a few pages to local groups that has fewer than twenty-five members. You can ask them to design you an online presence and then you'll need to pay the annual fee in order to make it available for use.

Volunteer for a non-profit.

One of the biggest challenges for photographers in a field that is competitive is finding an emotionally appealing photograph. Being a part of an organization that is non-profit is a cost-effective option to market your work. It doesn't matter what causes you are involved in or whether it's local or national, but look for something you're truly interested in. There are plenty of opportunities to get involved because many non-profit organizations are in need of your efforts just as you need the attention. It could be a local fund-raising event. Another option is an organization that utilizes a large number of photos for marketing or publishes a significant quantity of newsletters.

If you don't have the alternative to join an existing company, think about starting an individual campaign to address something that is important to you personally. Every region has a local problem that must be resolved. It may take a long time however, it will propel you into the spotlight. This Encyclopaedia of Associations lists all the most important associations in America Volunteering for Australia is the same website for Australia. These links will show the criteria to fulfill to be a member. It also assists in identifying a cause you would like to join. It is likely that other countries will keep that information, too. Make sure to check with your local library of reference as well as the Chamber of commerce.

Geography will, in some degree, determine the way this happens. It might be time-consuming to search to "save whales" when you're located in the middle of Australia however, there will be local environmental issues which needs to be dealt with. The benefits of working in your community is far more varied than keeping the public image. If you're involved in the community with a particular organization, it's possible to contact the local director of the group. While it is unlikely you'll receive an immediate commission however their approval of your work could permit you to use it as a marketing tool. This will also increase the amount of people who will speak of your project.

*It isn't unreasonable for youto, when you've completed a project and completing your work, to request an evaluation from a customer. It is not necessary to pay for this.

It could also mean that you'll be working together with experienced photographers and have the chance to learn new techniques.

It is possible to get film companies to provide you with the cost of the film as well as expenses for development, if the cause is of enough visibility. If this isn't an option you can consider, request for your suppliers in the area to support you. They will get the chance of publicity for free and also.

Volunteer Work

When you first begin marketing your photos it is likely that you'll spend more time on marketing rather than creating pictures. But, making sure your photos are noticed by prospective clients is crucial. Check out your local newspaper or, in the event that you see that there's a local charity or non-profit organization that is hosting an event, you can offer the professional photographer at no cost. Your time can be better spent at high-profile events, however getting recognized at all levels is the initial step to gaining recognition.

Another method to get your work noticed is to find local businesses to showcase your work. There's a lot of potential in this. Maybe the butcher in your town would like to show his clients how he cuts meat and would therefore require the photographer to capture images for display in the shop. Perhaps a local grocery store is going through major changes and is ready to show before and after pictures. Each of these suggestions can be useful to stay visible to the world even if you're working at your home. 30 years ago I ran an organization that was worth more than the value of a typical home. I made more money than my physician, however I couldn't get finance for a home because I was a self-employed. I was seen as an uninvolved flier regardless of the fact that my assets resulted in my wings being severely damaged. Things have changed however, this lingering feeling towards self-employed individuals is still present. These efforts will give you an image of an authentic person, which can boost your respect within the business community. A business cannot survive without respect and goodwill. Every person on the planet has had the experience of the image of a cowboy. Be sure that the image you portray is professionally.

Get your teeth gritted and pretend to be the next politician

Ask an elected official in your area to let you observe him for a few hours or a day.

Any elected official, at whatever level require more publicity than you've ever. You can also be sure that they will use this publicity to their greatest advantage. If you're willing capture the photos and they'll work to publish them. If you decide to select someone who has controversial opinions, ensure that you're in agreement with them in case you don't want to be embroiled in a backlash. The ideal time to make this decision would be before an election, specifically when the candidate does not appear like they will get reelected.

Chapter 13: Decorating Spaces With Photographs

In the majority of interiors, art photos are used to add a final finish.

It's one element that immediately warm the space to make it seem more like home.

Photographs can enhance the space emotionally and visually. They give us a view of the world around us, add an interest and a splash of color to wall space, and in general make the space more lively.

Here are some simple tips on about how to arrange pictures in a space.

In general, pictures should be placed in a way that the central point of the photo or grouping is about the eye level of the typical person. Although this may not be feasible in every circumstance,

It's a great guideline to remember.

Size and Grouping

* Convert image to wall size. Select smaller images for small walls, while larger pieces are ideal to fill large walls.

* Relate the photograph to the size of furniture. When hanging a frame photograph on a piece of furniture, it shouldn't be any longer than the length that the piece of furniture.

Do not hang the photos too close together or you'll result in a chaotic appearance. Do not hang them too far apart , or you'll lose the unified style.

The correct use of lines can help set the mood of an area:

The strong horizontal lines of a photograph or in the manner the picture is displayed, can be thought to relax and create the illusion of width the space.

The strong vertical lines of photographs or the arrangement of the wall can add to the illusion of height in the room.

Strong diagonal lines, either in a photograph by itself or as the form of a series of photographs placed on the wall can add the drama and intrigue.

* Utilize the symmetrical or asymmetrical arrangement of photos to create an informal or casual feel. Symmetry can add the formality and balance to an

arrangement. It is generally relaxing and pleasing to the person looking at it.

* A collection of photos ought to be considered as one unit

One big photo is a bold statement, and is simple.

* Multiple photographs mounted in one mat will give greater impact.

Themes

• Enhance the theme of your room by using photos, repeating the colors, patterns and styles of the interior.

Landscape photography visually opens the space. The distant view of the horizon can be viewed as a kind of window.

Color

The vibrant colors add energy to rooms, neutral colors tend to be more relaxing.

* Photographs will be more effective in generating impact when matted with a different color than the wall. Choose a mat with a darker shade to create a light-colored wall, and an easy mat for walls with dark colors.

Framing

*   Select frames and colors that complement the decor that you want to convey in your house.

* To coordinate a group of photos mat them and frame them together.

Lighting

*   Illuminate photographs well. It is possible to lose them if they are not properly illuminated.

* Depending on the area, it is possible to make use of a picture light track lighting, recessed or picture light lighting.

Hanging

* Hang photographs securely. Hooks are adjustable to how heavy the photo.

Care of Photographs

*   Never hang photograph in direct sunlight: it can fade.

* Do not place a photo above an open fireplace.

Don't hang photos on a wall outside with no insulation. It could dampen.

*   Keep a consistent humidity and temperature in the room.

Matboards and Adhesives need to be free of acid, or else it will be yellow.

Did You Have the Chance to Sell Your Photos? Part 1.

After spending a considerable amount of time taking photographs and building a vast collection of photos It is a difficult task trying to find a way to market your work.

With the right attitude and a lot of effort, you could see a profit for the time you've spent outside.

One of the easiest methods to start is by holding local galleries in your town hall, inviting your familyand friends and local businesses.

The first gallery is used as a place to learn. This is the place where you will make mistakes, but should take the lessons you learn from the mistakes. Your friends who understand will even laugh at your mistakes, but be aware that it's the beginning of a brand new business.

If you are selling prints through an art gallery, you shouldn't make any unnecessary assertions about the quality the prints. Offer suggestions regarding the proper good care of your prints for example, don't keep them in humid environments or expose them to the sun's rays. Make sure to print on good quality paper.

Make sure you choose the right time for hosting your first exhibit. Make sure you don't have it held in the beginning of January, as people tend to are spending a lot during the Christmas season and don't enjoy spending too much money in New Year. Choose a date when there are plenty of visitors visiting your city. Local pictures should be popular for tourists. Do not try to sell an image you think is "OK". If an image isn't appealing enough to hang it on your wall in your home, it's not suitable to be shown to the world.

There are many other ways to market your photos. Stock agencies need a minimum submission of 500-1000 images and regular submissions after that, but with little return. Sometimes it's better to do by yourself and promote your own work, particularly if you've had the ambition to become an expert in sales. There's no better location to begin than the town you live in with your first exhibit.

Once you have a feeling for the exhibitions, there's no reason not to visit other cities or towns. Gallery all over the world are always looking for photographer talent.

There is no rulebook for how to make a photograph sell. Sometimes, having them in the right location at the right moment can make a difference to a potential customer or client. Images are used all over the world to market ideas and products and there's no better place to begin then with your community.

If your photos are great enough to be included in contests or displayed in your home's walls you are sure to find them appealing enough to make them sellable.

Have you ever thought about selling Your Photographs Part 2?

Anyone who is able to make use of a camera in a professional manner is able to market their photos. Picture agencies deal with photographs of all subjects and are constantly looking for new talents.

Images libraries and stock agencies are involved in selling images. They don't offer advice on how you can take better pictures. Their goal is to make money selling images to book publishers, magazines as well as to the travel industry, and a myriad of other industries that rely on images.

A lot of photographers think of agency agencies only as an option option to sell their work. If you've been unable to market any of your photos there is a good chance that agencies won't take their work.

If you're interested in an agency that sells your photos and you are interested in selling them, you need to create high-quality images that are suitable for the market of agencies. Visit their website to see examples that are currently used.

If you believe your work is in line with their requirements and meets their requirements contact them via email or mail.

However, prior to putting your work in an agency you should make a list of agencies that are a good fit for your work. Send an email to each agency describing your work and the magazines that have published your work. If an agency is interested, they'll ask for examples.

If an agency has accepted you work for publication, please don't interpret this as a guarantee the images you submit will be sold.

Do not approach an agency until you've got a huge collection of photos. The initial submissions for minimums could range between 50 and 500 images and then regular submissions are needed after that. Many agencies operate on a commission basis , 50 percent is the most common fee. If an image is sold for 2100 euros, the photographer gets one hundred euros.

When an agency accepts photography work usually, they will need to have an initial four or five-year retention period. Agents typically offer reproduction rights to images - meaning that the photo is licensed to a buyer with the specified purpose.

It could take as much up to six months for an agency is able to sell the image belonging to you. The first step is to scan your photos when they're submitted via film. They then have to reach out to their customers and inform them that they have new images to be found. All taking time therefore you should consider supplying an agency for pictures as a long-term investment. It's only after you have a few hundred images stored in a library that you begin to experience regular sales.

Keep in mind that agencies aren't able to sell images if there's not an opportunity to sell them, and placing images with an agency isn't a guarantee of the sale.

Digital or film photography

The use of digital cameras has witnessed a phenomenal rise, but film is still an essential role of photography. It will be relevant for for a couple of years at minimum. Film has numerous advantages that photographers are still able to be aware of. Large players in the production of film such as Kodak is still investing in it millions of dollars, even though experts believe that digital film will be the dominant choice in the near future.

These are just a few of the reasons for why certain photographers would rather film over digital

1.) Facilities and Investment

People of all ages, not just photographers, have invested a lot in photography equipment that utilizes film. Cameras and lenses feature features that modern photography simply cannot compete with. When compared to a professional, high-end 35mm lens, a digital one isn't as advanced as traditional cameras are able to offer. If a photographer decides to go digital could end up spending more, particularly in the event that his lenses, flashes and other accessories aren't compatible with the latest digital camera.

2.) Wide Angle

The lack of wide-angle lenses, as well as the slow time to start up are just two of the major drawbacks of the most digital cameras. 35mm cameras are modified to digital cameras typically use an image sensor CCD which is smaller (usually approximately 245mm x 16mm) instead of those with a 36mm 35mm film, which results in narrow angles. Photographers who love wide angles might find the classic 35mm lens more to their preference.

3) Action

Film cameras can also provide an advantage in challenging photography situations. Contrary to digital cameras, which use batteries that can run out at the most inexplicably time and a 35mm camera is able to be switched on quickly and ready to use at any time you want to take a photo. In addition, digital cameras generally require several seconds to be ready for utilize it, which is clearly an issue for photographers that want to record actions that can't be replicated.

4.) Difficult Conditions

film cameras can be stronger cameras than digital ones and are able to withstand the harsh conditions that photography can require during the course of work. You can count on film to be much more secure than electronic particularly when working in poor weather condition.

5.) Comparing Costs

In terms of cost the advantages of film as well as digital and disadvantages differ based on the use. If you are a photographer with a budget of thousands of dollars per year could find a the digital camera more suitable. However, if you're not a professional photographer the income you earn may not be enough to cover the costs of switching to digital.

Printing Digitally: Simplifying Pixels and DPI's

Digital printing in photography has opened up new opportunities for professional and amateur photographers of all levels. For many photographers, the back-up of digital photography printing gives photographers the opportunities to take the best photos. Don't worry about the precious film and not being able to know for certain that there is anything worth capturing there!

When you're trying to get printing there are some items to be aware of to avoid the waste of high-quality photo paperand expensive printing ink. We'll go over some of the most basic terms related to digital photography. We'll also offer some tips for making the most effective prints.

Resolution

Resolution refers to the "image-sharpness of a document and is typically determined in dot (or pixels) per inch (DPI). It is also a reference to the sharpness of images that monitors and printers can reproduce. Based on the needs of your specific situation documents can be scanned in various resolutions. The larger the resolution of the document, higher the quality of the image and also the bigger the file will be.

When you are printing digital photos in your mind the first thing to make sure is to download your images at their highest resolution. If, at the end of the day, you've got 72dpi (dots per inch) images, then your printing quality will be a joke. A resolution of 72dpi is ideal to view on your monitor, but images with 200-300dpi is likely to produce an excellent quality 8x10 inch prints.

Pixel

Pixel is the abbreviation for Picture Element. The smallest element of a digital image and every image is made up of millions or thousands of pixels. The most basic unit, of where a video or computer image is created is simply just a dot, with a certain brightness and color. The larger the number of pixels an image contains more pixels, the greater the resolution will be. One Megapixel equals one million pixels

JPEG

Joint Photographic Experts Group (JPEG) is a standardization committee who designed this format for compression of images. The compression format that they created is referred to as a "lossy compression', since it removes data from images that it believes is unnecessary. JPEG files range from tiny amount of lossless compression, to huge quantities in lossy compression. It is a standard used on the World Wide Web, but the loss of data caused by the compression of JPEG files makes it unsuitable to print with.

When it comes to printing with digital photography it is usually done using images that are saved in the JPEG files format. Keep in mind that every time you save and open an JPEG file, you'll lose some of the information in the image. It is therefore recommended to make all changes at the same time and then save them just once.

Resolution Guide for High Quality Prints

The more pixels a camera can handle the more details an image will be preserved when printed or enlarged.

One to two Megapixels

Cameras with this resolution can be used to send photos electronically via email, however they aren't ideal to print photos. The majority of camera phones, PC camcorders, and even PC cameras have resolutions within the 1 to two megapixels range.

3-to-4 Megapixels

Cameras that offer this resolution can be used for printing and editing normal 4x6 inch image.

5 - to 6-Megapixels

Cameras that have this resolution can produce professional results when expanding photos to up to an 8x10 inch size.

7 Megapixels

Cameras that have a resolution with at minimum 7 megapixels will provide better quality and clarity when printing or enlarging images beyond the 11x14 inch dimension.

If you simply look at the file's size You will soon learn how to make an informed decision on the quality of the image. A photo that is 100kb (kilobytes) or less is probably low resolution for quality digital printing. When you reach the minimal size, which is 400kb or less then you're using a higher resolution for a print of 8x10 inches.

Printing Paper

If you are proud of your photography work, or would like your family photos to be preserved for the future generations You will certainly want your prints printed on a high-quality paper. It's no surprise that in the final your prints are only as excellent as the paper you're using.

There are numerous new coated papers in the market that are specifically designed for this purpose. You must consider the best paper for the printer you're employing.

The popular Archival paper, which is used among those who work with inkjet printing is the longest-lasting type of paper, and is also acid-free. Printing papers aren't inexpensive, so you must plan your purchases carefully. Print only after the final cropping or after the the completion of any other modifications for example, after the creation of a border by your image software.

Laser and regular color inkjet printers work well for charts and text, but not always the best choice for printing digital photos. PictBridge-equipped printers let you print digital photos directly from your camera. Printers that are portable, like HP

Photosmart 320 series, for instance. HP Photosmart 320 series, let you capture a photo and print 4x6 inch images anywhere you go.

For smaller prints, 4x6 inch dye-sublimation printers provide excellent high-quality prints and are usually waterproof. However, the supplies required for printing with dye-sublimation do not cost a lot!

If you are unable to achieve satisfactory results from your own printing of digital photos particularly if you're printing larger than 8x10 inches images, then you can consider one of the brick and mortar or online photo labs that use dedicated printers for photography that produce great results.

Photo labs are able to manage digital photos directly from memory cards. Bring your digital camera, an unofficial CD, or the memory card of your camera with you for professional printing of digital photos.

Do You Want To Start A Photography Business?

If you are a photographer, what could be more exciting than making it an income? Imagine how exciting it would be to get invited for a fee to many weddings or celebrations every year, to record precious family moments that will be cherished for a lifetime and to witness the children grow up and even enjoy seeing people smile each day during your job. Photography can help you achieve all this. And what is great about the photography industry is there's more than enough work for the freelance/work-at-home photographer.

For you to begin, you'll need to acquire the proper equipment. This requires you to establish the exact direction you'd like to expand your company. If you have a room at your home which you could make into an office, you may be interested in creating a backdrop as well as lighting equipment. However, perhaps you don't have space. Don't let this deter you. It is possible to be competitive in the field of photography even without having an office. One of the great things of a home-based photography company is that you are able to offer the same services that professional photographers provide however at less than the price. In addition, since you do not have to deal with expenses like rent and employees and you only need to focus on delivering high-quality images.

The good news is that taking quality pictures today is simpler thanks to the development of digital cameras. If you're on a budget, spending budget, you can begin with a home PC, digital camera and an above average printer. If your budget isn't too restricted, it's ideal to purchase some additional tools like camera filters or zoom lenses.

Chapter 14: The Best Way To Offer

Selling your work will only be able succeed if you are aware of what you want to sell. There are many options for selling prints as well as calendars, postcards and calendars digital images, as well as books. These are the categories of ways you can sell your photography, however "what you can sell" is more than the method you use to paste your image to buyers to purchase. The list goes on and on about mouse pads, mugs, dishestowels, kitchen gloves and many more. The problem of "what to offer" is not about the items however, it is the topic of the items.

It's all about understanding the people you are targeting.

Who is your intended audience?

Are you searching for top-quality buyers?

Are you trying to find buyers across the globe?

* What is your niche group you will sell to?

If you aren't able to answer questions regarding your intended market, you won't be able to market your work.

Did you see the elephant drawing artwork? There's a segment for this type of artwork. The target people "bleeding hearts" since the advertising is focused on how they can assist in taking the care of elephants who have been saved through buying an elephant-painted canvas.

What you consider to be important in your art work may not be what another considers important. It is important to be able to let go of your personal impression to be successful in selling your products.

What do you think about the photos you create will be valued by the buyer?

Perhaps your art is valued since the buyer is aware that in the next few years you'll sell your work for hundreds of dollars? It's probably not. The work you do touches them in a personal way. They feel a sense of ownership in your work as well as something that is touching them.

Let's take a look at Picasso for a while. Picasso created a whole movement he called "Cubism." The value of his work is in the number of geometric forms that are grouped together to form faces and other designs. The colors he uses in his work tend to be brown, red and similar hues, but they may also be extremely bright and incorporated to reveal the geometric picture that he created in his work. Do you like Picasso? Maybe, but you may also believe that a realistic picture like that of the Mona Lisa is hundred times superior to Picasso. Why? The answer lies in which kind of art appeals more to you than the other.

It is evident that you have some elements in your work that appeal to you. Landscape photographers are looking at the ocean, mountains and other areas surrounding them, trying to find an opportunity to display what is beautiful about it. It's the contrast between the light and shadows that enable a photographer to create an accurate depiction of what they are observing with their eyes.

Wildlife photographers are going strive to capture the events in the life of animals that are captivating to the viewers. For instance, a photographer taking photographs on safari might wish to see an lion eating something, taking a kill by openly showing teeth. Photographers who take photos of dogs or cats could attempt to document their adorableness. They could be selling calendars that feature cat images.

While you try to accomplish this, it's all done with the idea that is in your head that someone else will be able to discern what you see , or something else that makes it communicate to them.

When you are assessing your target market, you must be aware of what you can attract them and not just what you believe is likely to be popular simply because you like it.

What is the reason writers make the bestseller lists, if you don't like their writing style? This is because there is something about the story that makes them think beyond their writing style. It could be the marketing, or it could be the main subject or the plot.

Photographers need to recognize the worth in your work that another is looking at and decide if what you're selling will be successful in selling. It is possible that you will need to alter your subject matter to ensure they are marketed.

There is a good chance that you will require an impromptu trick. Let's take another look. You are a resident of an area that is a popular tourist destination. You've made the decision to earn profits selling postcards since tourists cannot get enough of the cheap items.

You make an image that depicts the largest mountain you can find in your region. It's your finest image and will beat out earlier photographers who were popular. The postcard is popular but it's just 10% of what is sold. A quick photo of a squirrel taking the nut is sold 60% more frequently. It's a mere five-second video and yet it's "too charming," and everyone must be able to have it. What you consider important does not mean that other people will be in love with. The cute squirrel you designed up can earn you money , not the mountain scenery that you spent hours trying to design.

Learning about the Competition

Another method to find out the products that are selling is to look at the competitors. It's a bit difficult online since you can find a fantastic website and it is among the top results of search engines. But that doesn't mean that they're actually generating sales. Users can browse a website without purchasing anything, and aid in its rise in the ranking.

If you're planning to study your competition, then you'll need to come up with an approach to determine what's selling. Photography makes it simple to look over the inventory that is not in inventory or listed as a best-selling item. Anything that is being sold or on clearance may be an advertising tactic or something that didn't sell.

The products that are the most difficult to purchase and receive in a short period of time are those which are sold on this particular website. It's similar to going into the gallery to see what's "sold" and what's not being sold. If you find a lot of pieces that are not mentioned as "sold" it might be a good idea to ask. Have they sold many items? Which is the most viewed work? If the gallery feels they'll generate revenue, they'll respond to your inquiries. Naturally, you must be a bit subtle when asking questions However, it is vital to know the market and what's hot in the marketplace. Like all artistic industries, what is popular will vary. The year one time it might be African landscapes while the next year it could be among the best 100 parks of national significance in the USA. The whole thing depends on current trends in home decor regarding what will be able to attract buyers.

Chapter 15: How To Properly Capture Images During Live Events

Once you're aware of in the effort required to become a professional musician and how using social media can be used to maximize the effort you're putting into now, we can concentrate on the specific ways you can earn money from the business of music photography. Although you're free to experiment with any of the methods described in the remainder part of this book it's crucial to realize that you'll likely succeed best when you focus on one particular area within the broad spectrum that's music photography. As an example instead of offering many different options to your customers, you might be known as the "guy who creates the most effective music video" or "the woman with the most impressive live concert pictures". The most effective rule of thumb is to start by testing photography in various ways, and then pick a method that is the most satisfying for you, because you'll feel confident that you'll be successful in your endeavor. This chapter will concentrate on ways to make your life as a concert photographer more enjoyable. Although this industry is highly competitive and there's no reason you shouldn't stand out from the crowd and make an exciting career path.

Step 1: Being a Live-Show Photographer: Begin with a small amount of experience.

It's certain that many top entertainers and performers got to their final aim of mass fame through small steps. As a photographer of music it is advisable to consider following this path. It's not wise to go into a big concert and try to be competitive with photographers who have many years of experience, while you're not even a little. You're likely to find that if planning to begin taking pictures for professional musicians, you have a few friends who is part of an ensemble. It's a good idea to inquire with them to photograph them at a show at no cost. It's highly unlikely that they'll say no. In addition, these events usually don't require you to wear specific badges for journalists in case you'd like to take your camera with you to the event. This is why it's a fantastic opportunity to try out your photography abilities.

Step 2 to Become an Live Show Photographer Make sure you purchase a speedy Lens Today!

If you've chosen the venue you're sure isn't crowded with competitive and skilled photographers mingling around it is advisable to purchase a speedy lens before the date of the concert. To comprehend what a speed lens can do it is essential to know the meaning of aperture. It's safe to say that you are aware of what an aperture means because you're fascinated by photography but for those who aren't the term aperture refers to an opening or a hole through which light can pass. For the camera an aperture is how big the aperture in side of the lens. The smaller aperture (or the f number) and the greater the light source as well as the camera's view hole. Although starting with a small location can be a fantastic opportunity to get experience but one of the main difficulties with starting out at smaller venues is the fact that lighting can be awful. Since the space itself is smaller it is focused on the performers and is not focused on showcasing the stage or any decorations behind it. While this can be great to create a more intimate atmosphere for the audience, it is not ideal for the aspiring musician photographer. It's highly likely that in these kinds of environments the photos you take are likely appear as if the person you're photographing has recently returned on Mars and is eager to begin a singing career.

A lens that is fast will permit more light to flow through lenses of cameras. This "fast" feature of this kind of lens is its shutter rate and a higher speed can help you get more light into your photo. If you're just starting out generally, it is recommended to purchase a cheap 50mm 1.8 lens as this type of lens lets you snap photos even when there is nearly absent. Another excellent tip to avoid any issues with tonal quality that arise due to the use of colored light sources is to render the photo black and white in edit. This can prevent the photo from appearing as if it was taken from another world, and then make it look normal. A low-cost but quick lens can help you save time in discontent and feeling that your photos taken at tiny venues do not come out exactly right.

Step 3 in becoming a Live Show Photographer: Change Your ISO Settings to High

ISO is the sensitiveness of the sensor in your camera, which detects an image. The higher the settings for sensitivity the more sensitive your camera's sensor is. That means the greater you go with the ISO settingis, the more capacity your camera will have to be able to see an image despite the darkness around it. In this case that you should use an extremely high ISO setting, in conjunction with a low f setting in your camera so that you can optimise the lighting of your photos even in dim illumination concert hall. The higher ISO settings can let you capture musicians without flash. This could be an advantage in an "no flash" venue for concerts. While ISO is a crucial concept for every photographer, it is important to recognize that the more you increase your ISO setting is, the less grainy the photo will appear. The grain you will see when using a high ISO setting is referred to in the world of photography in the photography world as "noise". To reduce the amount of noise you see, it's suggested to buy noise reduction software to do post-production editing once you've captured your images. These will help your photos stand out from other photos which look grainy and appear like they were taken by a novice.

Step 4: Being a Live-Show Photographer: Moving to the bigger venues

Some people may like the idea of beginning their photography career at a smaller venue while others may find it easier to get involved in the competition which is available at a bigger venue. Perhaps, you've worked at smaller venues for a long time, and you're now ready to go on to larger and more impressive things. Naturally the book strongly advocates that you should begin by gaining experience in smaller venues before making the move to larger venues however, regardless of the reasons behind this decision, there's one thing that is consistent within the realm of larger venues. It's that you'll probably need an invitation from a press agent to shoot in the location.

Don't panic! If you are able to do this through an internship, or by creating your portfolio and creating an online presence that can demonstrate that your qualifications as a professional photographer are valid The first step in the process is being associated with a larger business. This generally means representing magazines, radio station, a site or other website. Of course, you could attempt to portray yourself as an independent contractor to obtain the press pass however, this can be difficult. What the scenario where every venue permitted freelancers to take videos and photos during their events? There's a good chance there'd be more publicity than people if that was the scenario. If you reach out to these media outlets to inquire whether they're in need of an artist for their event, it's best to give them an email with a link to your site instead of Instagram or Facebook. Instagram. Websites look more professional over other platforms for social networking.

If you're unable to locate an outlet for media that can support you, don't to get discouraged. Instead, begin contacting others within the field who have connections at events. You may need to be more creative however the likelihood is higher that the greater number you reach out to the more likely to get someone to offer you access to an "in". Don't be afraid to step out of your comfort zone to achieve what you need. Don't get discouraged by the disappointing answer "no". If after trying these strategies, you're still not able to locate anyone who would like you to photograph an event, it's an opportunity to re-evaluate your work and determine what you can improve on. If you're looking to ask around for an invitation, you should reach out to the manager of the artist first, and then the PR manager of the venue next. In most cases, the manager is more powerful in comparison to the place.

Conclusion

Making money through selling photos online is a breeze no matter if you're an experienced professional or just starting out in this. With the advice and suggestions that are in this book, you'll have the guidance and support you require to launch your venture with less hassle and other issues.

There are bound to be difficulties and bumps in the road however, with determination and commitment to your profession you'll be able to show your talent and build a loyal following , and make money while doing it.

The author hopes that you'll be able to follow these steps starting with knowing how to begin your online photography business to choosing the most appropriate platform that you can utilize to sell the incredible photographs you've taken.

* 9 7 8 1 7 7 4 8 5 4 3 8 9 *